# The Fighting Tomahawk

This book is respectfully dedicated to my beloved wife, Jeneene, whose support and assistance have been a beacon of light guiding me home through the darkness and frustration that are so often found in the world of martial arts.

# The Fighting Tomahawk

## An Illustrated Guide to Using the Tomahawk and Long Knife as Weapons

### Dwight C. McLemore

Paladin Press • Boulder, Colorado

**Also by Dwight C. McLemore:**
Advance Bowie Techniques: The Finer Points of Fighting with a Large Knife
Bowie and Big-Knife Fighting System
Fighting Staff
Fighting Sword
Fighting Tomahawk: The Video

*The Fighting Tomahawk: An Illustrated Guide to Using the Tomahawk and Long Knife as Weapons*
by Dwight C. McLemore

Copyright © 2004 by Dwight C. McLemore

ISBN 13: 978-1-58160-441-2
Printed in the United States of America

Published by Paladin Press, a division of
Paladin Enterprises, Inc.
Gunbarrel Tech Center
7077 Winchester Circle
Boulder, Colorado 80301 USA
+1.303.443.7250

Direct inquiries and/or orders to the above address.

PALADIN, PALADIN PRESS, and the "horse head" design
are trademarks belonging to Paladin Enterprises and
registered in United States Patent and Trademark Office.

Visit our Web site at www.paladin-press.com

# CONTENTS

## BOOK 1: THE TOMAHAWK ⟵ 1

# BOOK 2: THE LONG KNIFE ⤙ 111

# BOOK 3: ENGAGEMENT SETS, SEQUENCES, AND RELATED FIGHTING CONCEPTS FOR THE TOMAHAWK AND LONG KNIFE ⤙ 175

# ACKNOWLEDGMENTS

Bryan Simpers of the Colonial Williamsburg Foundation and Richard Brown, executive director of Pricketts Fort State Park, just north of Fairmont, West Virginia, deserve special thanks for pushing this old wolf onto the path of the longhunter and of our colonial heritage.

Whenever embarking on a research project, one inevitably finds one or two special studies so insightful and profound that they become the road maps for the literary journey. In this endeavor there were two such sources that enabled me to "see" the true applications of the tomahawk and the impact of both culture and environment on its use. The door-opening studies for me were Mark A. Baker's *The Sons of the Trackless Forest* and Wayne Van Horne's doctoral thesis, "The Warclub: Weapon and Symbol in Southeastern Indian Societies."

Baker's masterful application of both first- and secondhand accounts, supplemented by his application of "experimental archaeology," gave me the "feel" of how both the Indians and the white men actually used the tomahawk in the age of the single-shot firearm. As I worked with this text, I saw, with a longhunter's eyes, the need for the tomahawk as both a tool and an essential backup weapon. The section on train-ing in 18th-century America was a key in supporting my theories on the migration of fighting techniques from Europe during the period of colonization.

Van Horne's dissertation on the war club provided me the view of tomahawk-like combat from the perspective of the American Indian. His expansion of first-person accounts from both Spanish and English expeditions painted a clear picture of how the use of the war club led to the adoption of the tomahawk by Indian cultures. The role of the war dance as a primary training vehicle by the Indian tribes was also reinforced by this invaluable work.

Finally, the greatest lesson from both authors is the value of oral history and first-person accounts in documenting lost fighting arts. I can never repay these authors for their service; all that can be said is thanks.

# WARNING

**M**isuse of the information and techniques in this book could result in serious injury or death. The author, publisher, and distributor of this text disclaim any liability from damage or injuries of any type that a reader or user of the information may incur. The techniques should never be attempted or practiced without the direct supervision of a qualified weapons instructor. Moreover, it is the reader's responsibility to research and comply with all local, state, and federal laws and regulations pertaining to possession, carry, and use of edged weapons. This text is for *academic study only*.

# PREFACE

I cannot guarantee that what you find in this book is authentic tomahawk and long-knife techniques of the 18th and 19th centuries. To date I have found no individual manual or text that qualifies for this honor. All that can be said is that more than 180 hours of full-speed assault practice and countless hours of research went into this text. I have explored many first-person interviews and accounts of the American colonists and colonial militia engagements with the Indians, as well as journals from the French and Indian Wars and the accounts of assaults on various forts of the period. Late medieval and Renaissance manuals were also consulted to form the protocol for techniques that may have migrated to America during the period of exploration.

When one considers authentic historical fighting methods, the bottom line is that we are all just guessing. We didn't live in those periods and therefore didn't actually see or experience the hazards that everyday living brought. Much of the training then was far different than the task-organized methodologies of today's soldiers, law enforcement officers, and martial artists. Training systems as we think of them today did not exist. Particularly on the frontier, much of the training was passed on through word of mouth, personal notes, or observation. Sometimes this was as simple as a grandpa explaining to his grandson the difference between chopping wood and splitting a skull in self-defense, or as complex as practicing reloading a muzzleloading rifle on the run.

Where there were gaps in my research, I attempted to fill in with logic and commonsense applications that I think a person of those times would have used when preparing to defend his family in the wilderness. My focus for this document is heavily oriented to those areas east of the Mississippi River. The use of the tomahawk in the American Southwest is a subject for another book.

The Web sites cited were current at the time of publication.

—Dwight C. McLemore
May 2004

# The Tomahawk

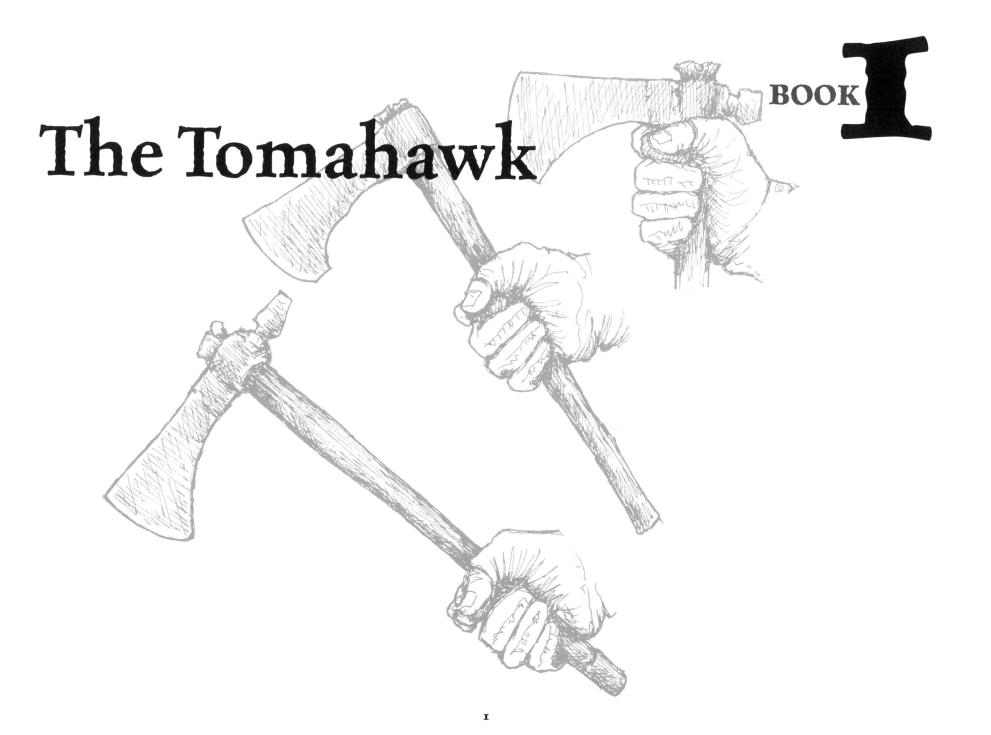

## BOOK I

# PART I
## The Basics of the Tomahawk

# An Attempt at a Historical Background

The fighting arts in North America of the 17th, 18th, and early 19th centuries do not entirely follow or parallel their forms in the British Isles and continental Europe of those times. And we are not sure that we can trust the traditional descriptions and explanations of the arts, often mythological, that were developed after the fact.

We do have some written sources that are sometimes relevant to the subject, and it is safe to say that some first-person oral accounts tell a true tale.

So the training techniques in this book obviously cannot be authenticated. They are the result of understanding that the human body can be made to perform only so many actions. They are also based on common sense, which was essential to what the settlers of colonial America were trying to accomplish in their lives—just as their forebears in the Old World had done for centuries.

The colonists were prepared to be "fighting men." They possessed firearms and often swords of one kind or another. Their axes and knives could serve as either tools or weapons. In the colonies of North America were to be found many veterans of the seemingly endless wars of the Old World of the time, and many of the settlers came from rural societies that were normally violent (not something we'd think of today). Those who had the implements, as did almost all, knew how to use them.

## THE HATCHET OR THE TOMAHAWK

Ever since humans first figured out how to make and use tools, the hand ax in one form or another has been used for splitting skulls or pieces of wood for kindling. (The large ax came much later.) The hatchet (from the French *hachette,* "small ax") was regularly issued to the elite grenadier units, for instance, of the British army of the 17th and 18th centuries; they functioned as the commando or combat engineers of the time and were expected to break into flimsy enemy field fortifications quickly. No doubt the hatchets were sometimes used at close quarters when the grenades and muskets wouldn't quite do. The rest of the time the hatchets were used in the same way that civilians employed them: for firewood and hacking up tough cuts of meat.

The hatchet, made of steel, was an instant success among the indigenous peoples of the eastern parts of North America, and they were manufactured as quickly as possible for trade purposes. These little axes took on forms that would not be quite recognizable in Europe (e.g., the tobacco pipe as part of the head) but were very useful and pleasing to their American Indian beneficiaries.

Among the military units in the British colonies of North America the hatchet was common, for obvious reasons. And it did become popular among the settlers, as well as the British regulars posted to the colonies. During the Seven Years War (locally the French and Indian War) of 1756–1763, among others, the individual colonies were raising militia units and trying to equip them. Although militia members wished very much to be outfitted like regular troops with musket, bayonet, and sword (or "hanger," often a popular cutlass-like affair), some colonies' published militia regulations specified that "tomahawks" would be supplied in place of swords—or even bayonets—because such blade weapons were in very short supply in the colonies.

European regular army regiments formed special light infantry units to operate in the wild lands and wars of the 18th-century colonies, and among other clothing and equipment modifications, they made sure they had their tomahawks.

It's a sure thing that the tomahawk came into play as a close-quarter weapon when all else had failed. The long knife was definitely used in close-quarter combat, just as it had always been in brawls, and occasionally in battle, in the Old World. It seems that there may be some substance to James Fenimore Cooper's *The Last of the Mohicans*.

Let's train!

# Chapter 1

# HISTORY OF THE TOMAHAWK

From the earliest centuries of European invasion and settlement, the use of edged weapons in North America paralleled that in Europe; the sword and knife remained popular sidearms. However, change was in the wind. By the late 17th century, halberds and partisans had become symbols of military rank rather than fighting weapons. Pikes were dropped from the militia inventory; the lance was kept only by some European cavalry units.

Traditionally, the tomahawk was associated with the North American Indian. The word *tomahawk* is derived from the Algonquian *tamahakan* and refers to the use of any type of striking weapon: wooden war clubs and stone-headed axes were in this category. When the tribes began to acquire hatchets from European traders, naturally this term was applied to these new weapons. If an Indian owned a small trade ax, he called it a "tamahak." As soon as the traders heard this, the market for the "tomahawk" was born. But the vast majority of tomahawks were made by either European or colonial smiths, and very few were produced by the Native Americans.

## THE ANATOMY OF THE TOMAHAWK

From the period of the French and Indian Wars to well past the American Revolution, some colonial militias required the sword, bayonet, or tomahawk as the soldier's sidearm. Even as the sword passed from common use, the tomahawk continued to be carried because of its usefulness as a tool, if nothing else.

The tomahawk was notable because of its ease of maintenance and its durability. Its head was virtually unbreakable, and usually only a file or stone was all that was required to maintain a functional edge. An occasional application of oil or grease was sufficient to prevent rusting. Even under the most extreme treatment, the handle was usually all that required replacement. Whether you were throwing it or banging it around doing farm chores, the "hawk" was always ready to function as a weapon.

The head of the tomahawk was especially versatile. In addition to cutting, the top could be used for thrusting. The back (hammer or pipe) could function as a mace or club. The tomahawk could be thrown up to 50 feet, and the weight of the weapon alone was sufficient to drop an enemy whether hit by the edge, hammer, or handle. The close-quarter combat characteristics of the tomahawk were also impressive. Holding the weapon with the hand halfway up the handle allows the delivery of close-range slashes with the edge. This grip also extends the handle for clubbing or thrusting. Perhaps the tomahawk's greatest advantage is the ability to use the downward curve or hook of the head to pull or trap an opponent's limb or weapon.

The tomahawk has three disadvantages: (1) the tapering handle

## HEAD DESIGNS OF THE COMMON TOMAHAWK

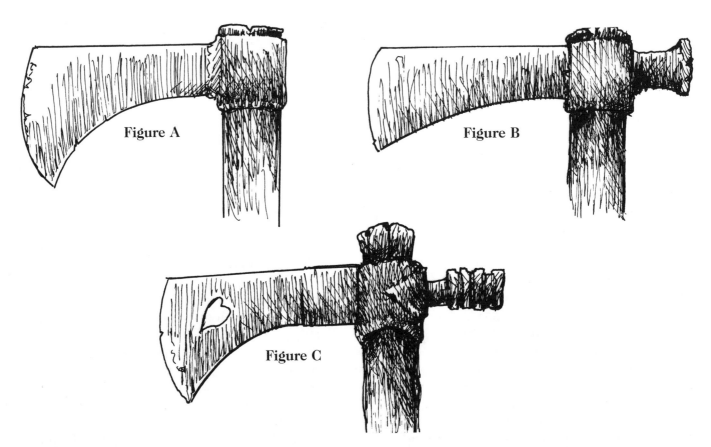

Figure A

Figure B

Figure C

makes the weapon difficult to hold if a target is missed; (2) closely related, the heavy head and gravity combine to make some strikes very expansive and therefore difficult to recover from should they be missed and the enemy counterattacks; and (3) the handle of the tomahawk can be easily broken if it strikes a heavier weapon.

Depicted above are the head designs for the three tomahawks seen in this book. Figure A is a rifleman's belt ax from the northern New York area before the Revolutionary War. Figure B is a hammer poll tomahawk made in France around the 1760s. Figure C is a pipe

tomahawk from the late 1700s. The techniques in this text can be performed with most any ax or tomahawk-like weapon. Even Indian war clubs can be used.

The handles of tomahawks during this period varied greatly in length and size. The average handle length was about 16 inches from the end of the handle to the tip of the head. The handles of some were up to 19 inches. The longer handle was probably chosen to enhance the leverage needed for various chopping chores. Some common tomahawks are shown on the following pages for comparison.

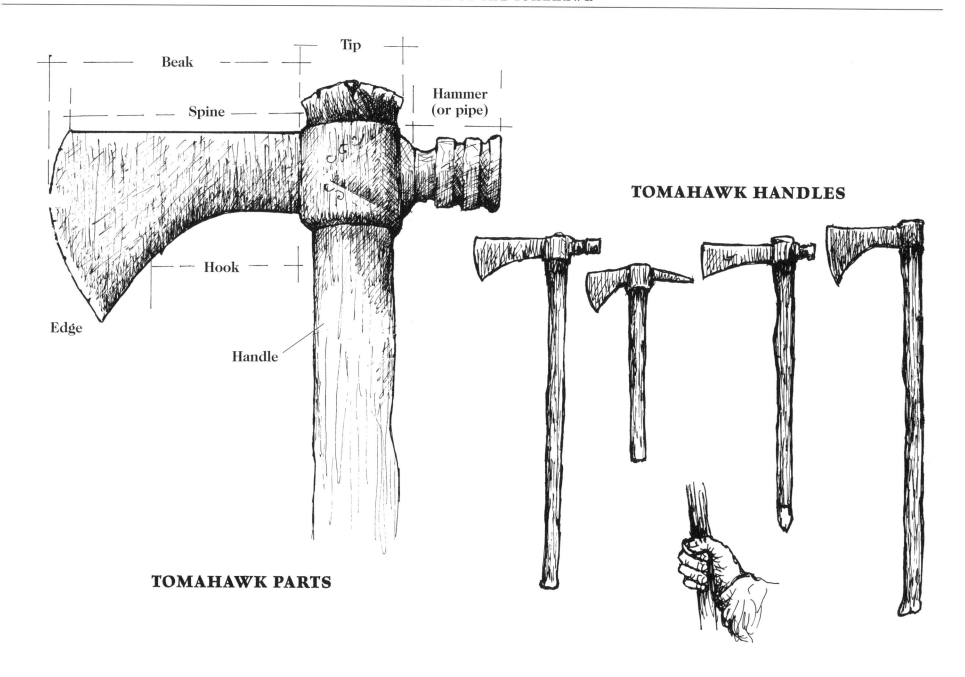

Beak

Tip

Spine

Hammer
(or pipe)

Hook

Edge

Handle

**TOMAHAWK HANDLES**

**TOMAHAWK PARTS**

# Chapter 2

# GRIPS

T here is no single correct way to grip the tomahawk. Strength, hand size, weight of the head, and distance to the target all have an impact on the grip to be used. In this book we are concerned with two grip factors: the position of the fingers around the handle and the placement of the hand on the handle.

There are two basic grips for the tomahawk: extended and hammer. Either grip may be used with three basic holds on the handle: the long position (holding the tomahawk by the end), the half-choke (holding it halfway up the handle) position, and the full-choke position (holding it with the hand immediately against the head of the weapon). Determining which grip is appropriate depends on how the cutting head of the tomahawk is presented. The cut or slash with the tomahawk head involves the edge's slicing through a target, much like that of a knife or saber. The chop with a tomahawk penetrates the target instead of cutting through it. The effective grip for a slash is the extended grip; the best grip for a chop is usually the hammer grip. From the aspect of hand position, both grips may be used in the three basic positions on the handle: the long, half choke, and full choke. The next few diagrams depict these grips and positions to perform slashes and chops.

## EXTENDED GRIP

This grip maximizes the delivery of the slash. Hand positions

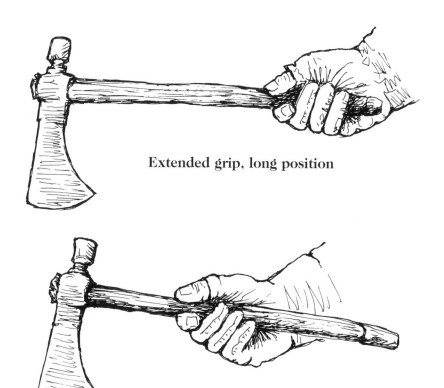

Extended grip, long position

Extended grip, half-choke position

that facilitate this grip are the long and the half-choke positions. The long position is normally used for medium-range combat, while the half choke is for close quarters.

## HAMMER GRIP

The hammer grip maximizes the delivery of the chop. Hand positions that facilitate this grip are the long choke, half choke, and full choke. The long position is normally used for medium range, whereas the half choke and full choke are best for close quarters. Both the chop and slash can be delivered from the full-choke position, and the extended handle can also be used as a striking element.

Hammer grip, full-choke position

Hammer grip, half-choke position

Hammer grip, long position

# Chapter 3

# STANCES

The selection of a fighting stance is purely a matter of personal preference; you should use the one that is most comfortable. Remember that in both single and multiple combat the stance is only a place from which to start an offensive or defensive action. It is not a static position but rather one that a fighter comes back to when there is a lull in the engagement. Some factors to consider when selecting a stance are the following:

- From any stance you must be able to move quickly laterally, forward, or to the rear to either attack or avoid an attack.
- You must maintain your balance or center of gravity. Shorter people may find that they are more comfortable with the wider, deeper stance, while those who are taller may prefer a more upright stance with their feet closer together.

- When you are in the middle of the battlefield or an ambush, there is little time to draw your weapons and assume a stance. All practice should emphasize drawing the tomahawk both in and off balance and going immediately into the attack. Remember, the tomahawk and long knife are basically backup weapons to be used when firearms misfire or cannot be reloaded. In these situations only a fool would assume that an attacking enemy will give him time to assume a stance. Train accordingly.

There are three fundamental stances that lend themselves to tomahawk use: the strong-side-forward stance, weak-side-forward stance, and frontal stance.

## STRONG-SIDE-FORWARD STANCE

To assume the strong-side-forward stance, stand straight with feet shoulder-width apart and on line. Rotate the left foot approximately 10 degrees to the left and move it back to the rear about 12 to 15 inches. Move the right weapon arm up to a half-chamber position and hold the tomahawk slightly forward in either a hammer or an extended grip. (**NOTE:** Movements are exactly the opposite for left-handed fighters.)

## ASSUMING THE STRONG-SIDE-FORWARD STANCE

1. Start in a frontal stance.

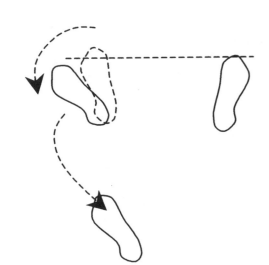

2. Shift the left foot approximately 10 degrees to the left. Step back 10 to 15 inches.

# WEAK-SIDE-FORWARD STANCE

To assume the weak- (or knife-) side-forward stance, stand straight with feet shoulder-width apart and on line. Rotate the right foot approximately 10 degrees to the right and move it back to the rear about 12 to 15 inches. Move the right weapon arm back to full-chamber position. Extend the knife or the empty hand forward, slightly flexed in either a saber or reverse grip.

### Assuming the Weak-Side-Forward Stance

1. Start in a frontal stance.

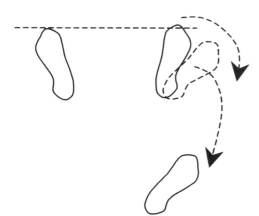

2. Shift the right foot approximately 10 degrees to the right. Step back 10 to 15 inches.

## FRONTAL STANCE

The frontal stance is used primarily when you are armed with a weapon in each hand. Basically, the torso is turned toward the opponent with the left or right leg pulled back approximately 6 inches for balance. Weapons can be held in extended arms with a slight flex and parallel to each other in front of the torso. Another application is with either the right or left weapon held back (high or low).

# Chapter 4

# GUARDS

W hile the stances are of primary concern with foot position, the guards are mostly concerned with the arm and hand positions. As with the stance, the guards are not firm, fixed positions but rather positions from which an engagement is begun or returned to during lulls in the fighting. Stances and guards work together to provide the maximum protection possible.

The primary aspect for any guard is the position of the arms. There are basically three positions in which the arms may be held when assuming any guard or stance: extended, at half chamber, and at full chamber.

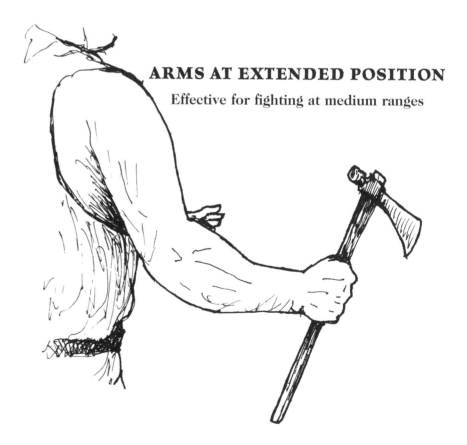

## ARMS AT EXTENDED POSITION
Effective for fighting at medium ranges

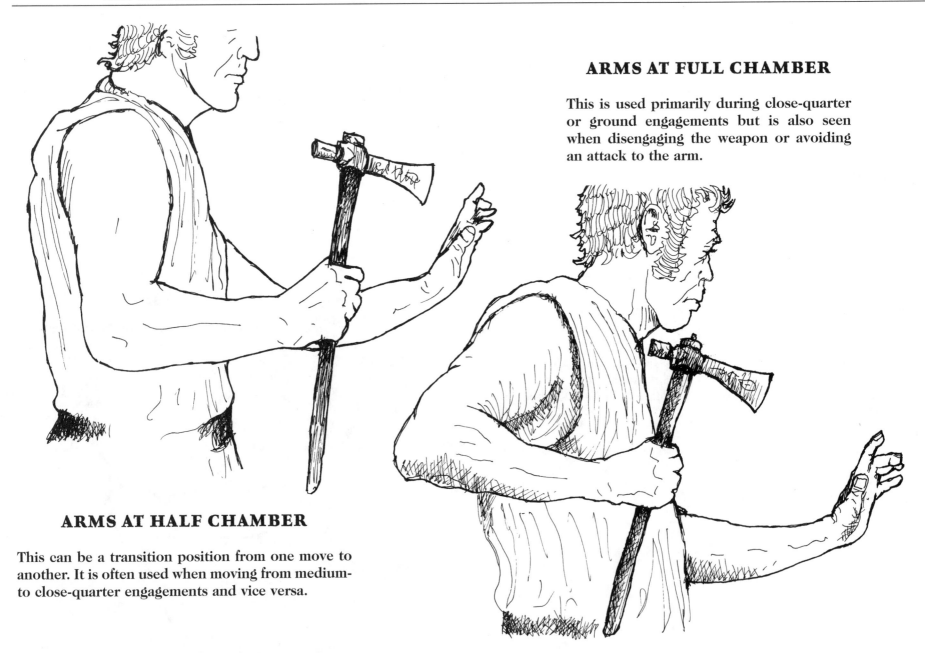

## ARMS AT FULL CHAMBER

This is used primarily during close-quarter or ground engagements but is also seen when disengaging the weapon or avoiding an attack to the arm.

## ARMS AT HALF CHAMBER

This can be a transition position from one move to another. It is often used when moving from medium- to close-quarter engagements and vice versa.

Three common guards are associated with the stance: high, middle, and low. As with stances, guards are simply positions from which to begin an engagement and return to during a lull in the fighting. The guard used depends on the type of weapon your opponent has and the manner in which he presents it. The three guards are discussed more in the section on fighting scenarios.

Tomahawk in middle guard and
long knife in middle guard

Tomahawk in high guard and
long knife in middle guard

Tomahawk in low guard and
long knife in middle guard

# Chapter 5

# DRAWING THE TOMAHAWK AND LONG KNIFE

The technique of drawing is directly tied to the carrying position, which is a matter of personal preference. Historically speaking, it seems there was a trend for three carry positions: the left-side carry, the right-side carry, and the back carry. In this chapter we'll see how the tomahawk and long knife are drawn into action.

The left-side carry appears to have originated in the military before the French and Indian Wars. The source may have been the French and English sword belt with a "frog," which was used for carrying swords and bayonets. Evidence indicates that frogs were modified to carry a tomahawk or hatchet. Earlier inventories and drawings indicate that this was a common practice with, among others, the French marines. Equipment records for elements of George Washington's colonial army indicate that such harnesses were virtually nonexistent among colonial militias and frontier riflemen. From these records we can infer that only those individuals with experience in the European armies of the 1700s retained the habit of a left-side carry, probably with a standard waist belt without the frogs.

Source paintings and drawings also reinforce the theory that right-side and back carry were common to longhunters, frontiersmen, and Indians.

In all three carry positions, the location of the long knife in relation to the tomahawk provided options: tomahawk and long knife together on the same side, tomahawk on one side and long knife on the other, and so on. Although this text details only three of the options, you are encouraged to explore the possibilities to find the one that best suits your skill level.

## LEFT-SIDE CARRY

The two illustrations on the following page show a British and a French sword and bayonet belt from the late 17th and mid-18th centuries. For our training purposes the tomahawk and long knife are positioned together on the left side as depicted in the second illustration.

## HISTORICAL NOTES ON TOMAHAWK AND LONG KNIFE CARRY

"On discharging his piece, he was attacked by several indians at once; the first [who] made up to him he knocked down with his gun, but the savages wresting it out of his hand, he knocked down another with a tomahawk which he carried under his belt."

—*Pennsylvania Gazette*, October 6, 1763

"The belt, which was always tied behind, answered several purposes, besides that of holding the dress together. In cold weather the mittens, and sometimes the bullet-bag, occupied the front part of it. To the right side was suspended the tomahawk and to the left the scalping knife in its leather sheath."

Rev. Joseph Doddridge, 1763–1783
Notes on the settlements and Indian Wars
of western parts of Virginia and Pennsylvania

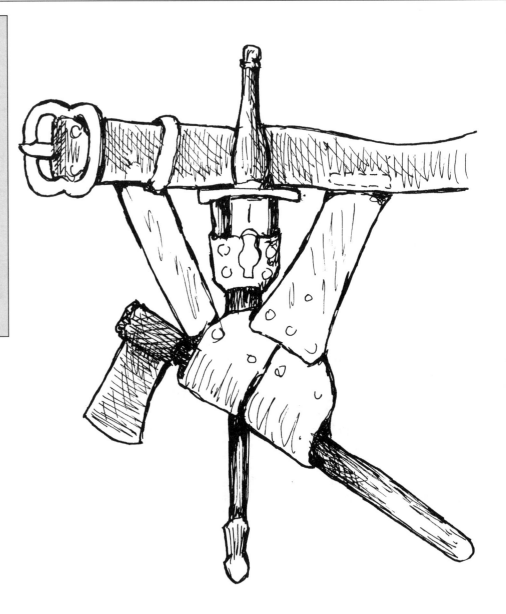

French infantry enlisted man's
belt from the late 1600s

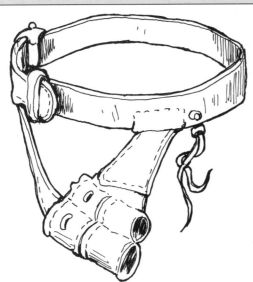

British sword and bayonet belt ca. 1751
(as in David Morier's paintings)

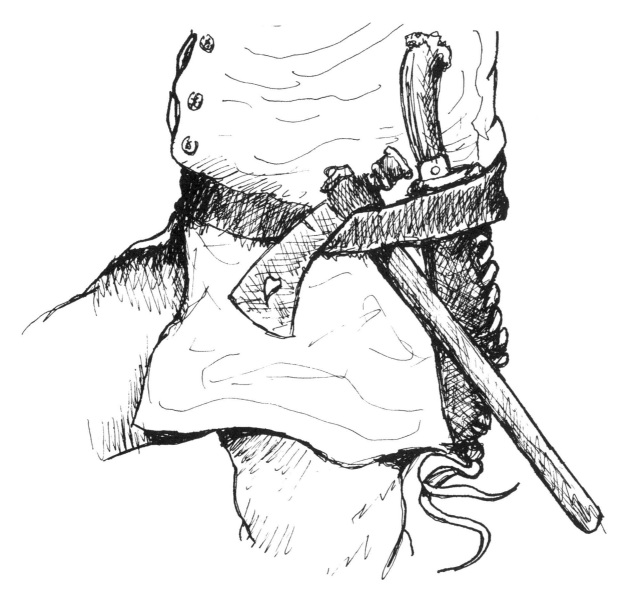

Left-carry position for the colonial frontier from 1731 to 1778

# TOMAHAWK AND LONG-KNIFE DRAW FROM LEFT-SIDE CARRY

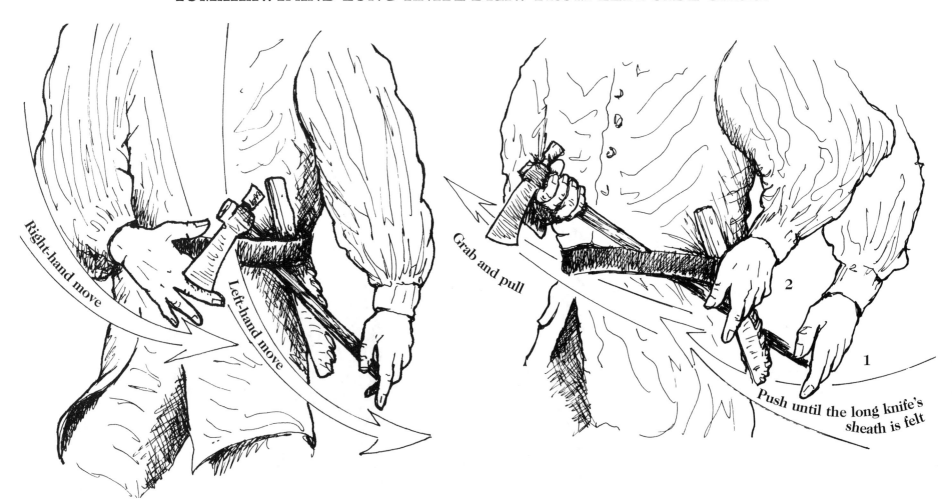

**Action 1:** Left hand swings down following the contour of the torso around to the butt end of the tomahawk.

**Action 2:** Right hand swings across the stomach and under the beak of the tomahawk. Simultaneously the left leg steps out and passes to the rear, arriving in a strong-side-forward stance.

**Action 3:** The left hand pushes the tip of the tomahawk forward and out of the belt. The right hand grasps the tomahawk in a full-choke grip below the head.

24

**NOTES:**

1.  The long knife may also be drawn using the saber grip, but this requires the rotation of the left hand clockwise toward the body over the knife handle to secure the grip. It also requires the blade to be pulled free of the sheath and rotated counterclock- wise to put it into action. Much training is needed to acquire the skill and timing to bring the weapon into action rapidly.

2.  The advantages for drawing the long knife in reverse grip are ease of control and speed of action.

3.  Both the reverse and saber grip should be practiced as part of the training regimen.

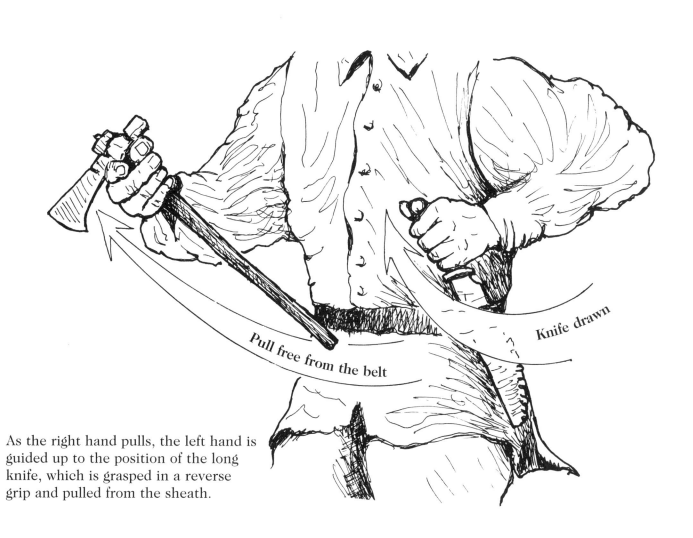

Pull free from the belt

Knife drawn

**Action 4:**  As the right hand pulls, the left hand is guided up to the position of the long knife, which is grasped in a reverse grip and pulled from the sheath.

1. Hammer grip, full choke

2. Back on hip

3. Slide hand back to half choke

**Action 5:** Bring the tomahawk and long knife into a middle- or high-guard position. The tomahawk is still held with a full-choke grip; to adjust to another grip, simply drop the handle end back onto the hip and slide the hand to the desired grip.

**NOTE:** Practice the draw regularly with 10 to 15 repetitions of the complete sequence. As your skill increases, combine the draw with the attack sequences (covered later) from a variety of upright, kneeling, sitting, side, and supine positions. When an opponent is closing rapidly, a speedy draw is essential.

## RIGHT-SIDE CARRY

The right-carry position was prevalent on the American frontier between 1731 and 1778. This illustration shows the common carry of the tomahawk on the right and the long knife on the left.

### Description of the Tomahawk and Long-Knife Draw from Right-Side Carry

Action 1:   The right hand swings down following the contour of the torso and grips the tomahawk just below the head. The tomahawk is then pushed forward and up, clearing the belt.

Action 2:   Simultaneously, the left hand reaches down and back, securing a reverse grip on the long knife and pulling up and out. The left or right leg can be passed forward or backward to assume either a strong- or weak-side-forward stance.

NOTE: Here the long knife is carried on the left side and the tomahawk on the right. As with the left-side carry, the long knife can be positioned on the right with the tomahawk, requiring a cross reach with the left hand. The disadvantage is that the arm reaching across can be easily trapped or pinned by a rapidly closing opponent.

TRAINING NOTE: Practice the draw regularly with 10 to 15 repetitions of the complete sequence. As skill increases, combine the draw with the attack sequences covered later from a variety of upright, kneeling, sitting, lying on either side, and supine positions. When an opponent is closing rapidly, a speedy draw is paramount.

Left side

Right side

## ACTIONS 1 AND 2

## ACTIONS 3 AND 4

NOTE: The visualizations of actions 1–6 (on this and the following page) demonstrate the draw when the tomahawk and long knife are carried on separate sides.

## ACTIONS 5 AND 6

5
Brace

6
Shift hand to grip

## BACK CARRY

Another popular carry position among the longhunters had the tomahawk on the right back and the long knife on the left back. This was usually seen when the "possibles bag" (a slang term for the large leather pouch carried by 18th-century longhunters) and the powder horn were on the left and the pistol on the right. Carrying a dagger or knife at the back dates to well before the Renaissance and can be seen in Marozzo's drawings of a left-handed dagger. The order in which the tomahawk and long knife are drawn is a matter of personal choice and often depends on the closeness of the opponent and which arm may already be engaged. The next three action views depict the draw from the back carry. This particular carry is one of the few options that facilitates the draw with a saber grip. All others that are depicted are best suited for the reverse-grip draw.

## ACTION 1

**Action 1:** The right hand swings back, following the belt line, and secures the tomahawk under the head.

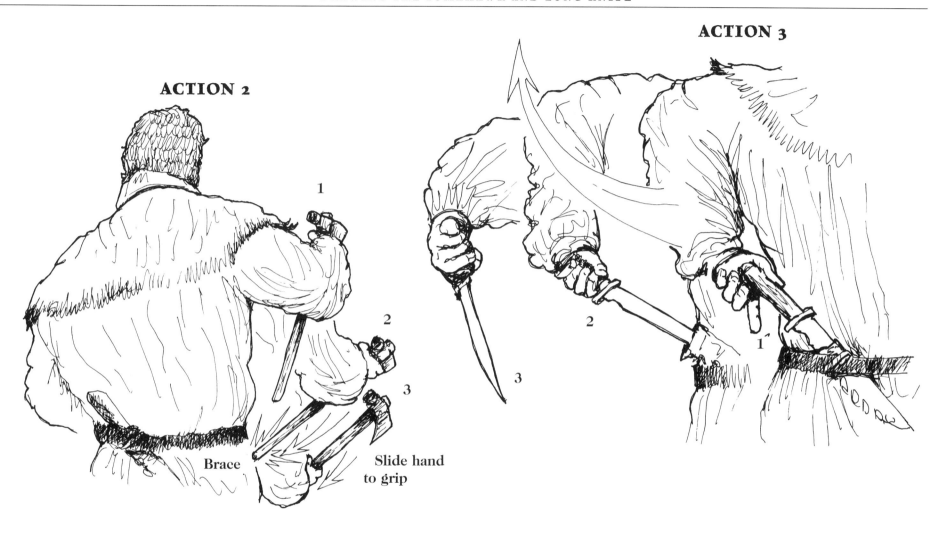

**ACTION 2**

Brace

Slide hand
to grip

**ACTION 3**

**Action 2:** Pull the tomahawk handle free of the belt and immediately push it back against the hip. With the tomahawk stabilized against the hip, loosen the grip and slip the hand back to the desired grip on the handle.

**Action 3:** With the tomahawk clear, swing the left hand back along the belt line and grasp the long knife in a saber grip, bringing it to the guard position.

# PART II
## Offensive Use of the Tomahawk

# Chapter 6

# THE CUT

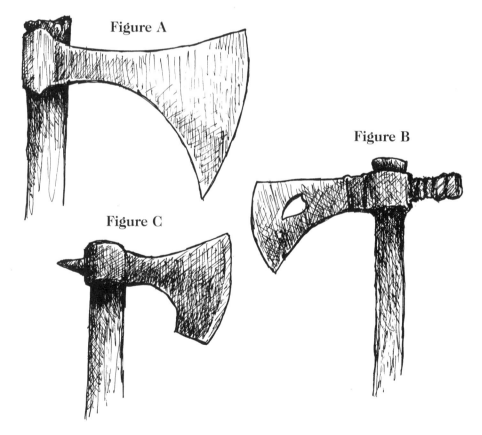

Figure A

Figure B

Figure C

The next few chapters involve the employment of the tomahawk on the offense. For our purposes there are three primary modes of attack: the cut, the chop, and the punch with the head of the weapon.

The cut is a smooth-flowing action in which the edge of the tomahawk beak strikes and is pulled through the target area in a way similar to that used with a big knife or cutlass. Normally, the edge passes uninterrupted through the target without the hook's catching on the target; the action should flow smoothly, almost immediately, into another cut or action. The cut produces a wide, deep wound that is very effective in severing ligaments. The ability to judge the distance accurately and make a proper presentation of the edge is essential for delivering accurate cuts. Because the edge is forward of the axis line of the handle, it is easy to misjudge distance when delivering the cut along the arc of a swing. Familiarity with the shape of the tomahawk beak is imperative.

Because there are many tomahawk and ax designs that can be used in the manner described, it is critical to understand how shape can influence effectiveness. Here is a general rule: those weapons with wide beaks and curved edges will deliver smooth cuts. Figures A through C depict tomahawk-ax designs that produce effective cuts.

## VISUALIZATION OF THE CUT

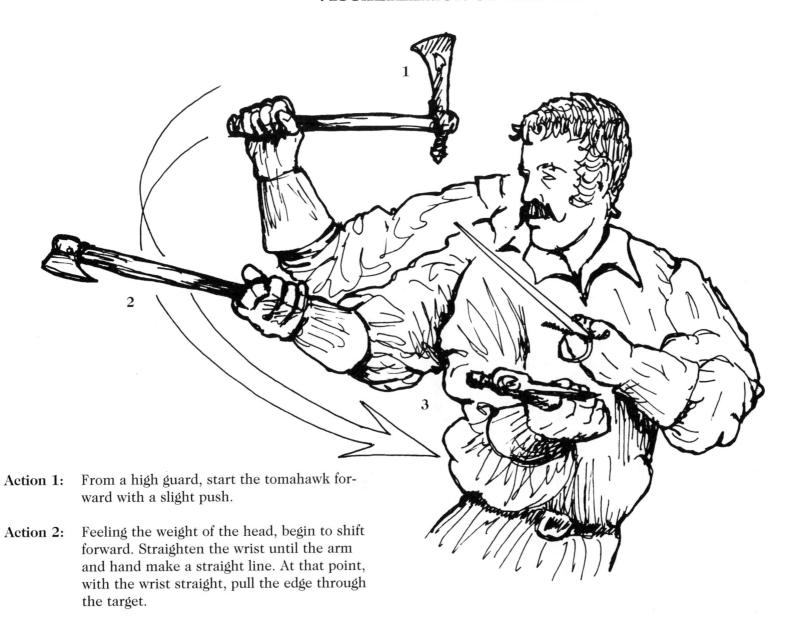

**Action 1:** From a high guard, start the tomahawk forward with a slight push.

**Action 2:** Feeling the weight of the head, begin to shift forward. Straighten the wrist until the arm and hand make a straight line. At that point, with the wrist straight, pull the edge through the target.

# Chapter 7

# THE CHOP

The chop is an abrupt hacking motion in which the edge of the tomahawk beak is impeded in the target area. Because the motion is interrupted on impact, usually the weapon must be retracted in the opposite direction to free it for another attack. The chop produces deep, wide wounds and is quite effective in cleaving though bone and ligaments.

Some beak shapes produce more effective chops than cuts. Normally, tomahawks with narrow, straight beaks and straight edges are best suited for delivery. Figures C and D depict two of these shapes.

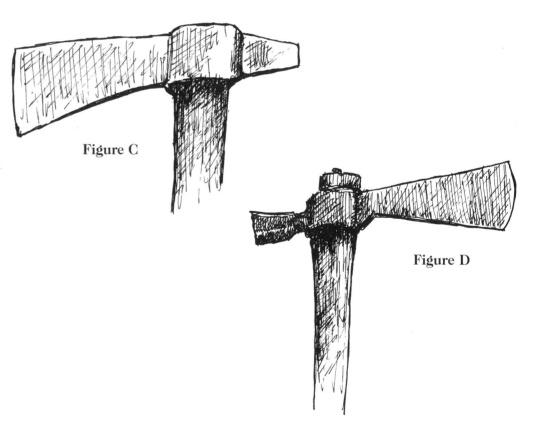

**Figure C**

**Figure D**

## VISUALIZATION OF THE CHOP

The major difference between the chop and the cut rests with the position of the hand in relation to the arm on impact. With the cut the wrist is extended; with the chop it remains at a 5-to-8-degree angle from the arm, as depicted below.

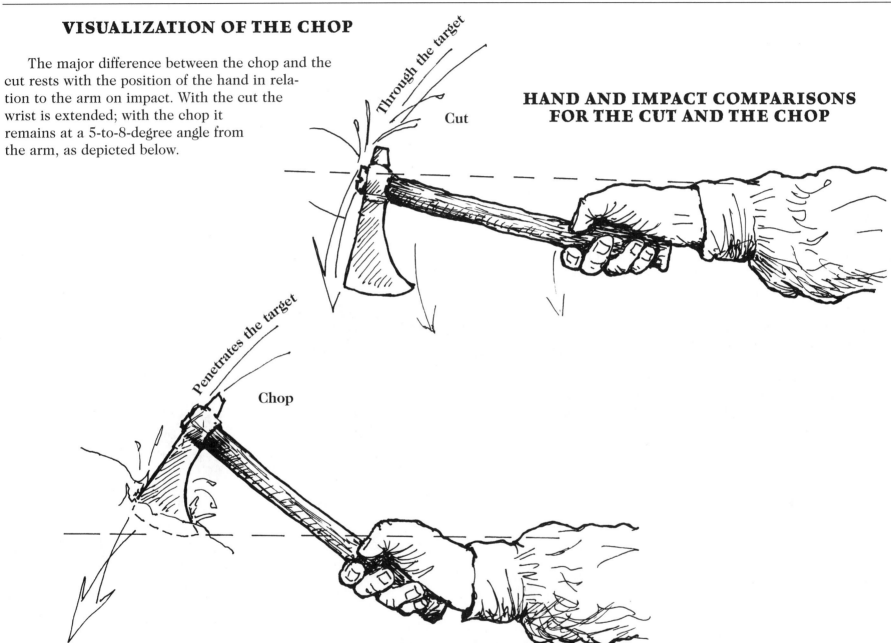

Through the target

Cut

## HAND AND IMPACT COMPARISONS FOR THE CUT AND THE CHOP

Penetrates the target

Chop

## VISUALIZATION OF THE DOWNWARD OVERHAND CHOP

## FRONTAL CHOP VISUALIZATION

# Chapter 8

# FLOURISHING DRILLS FOR THE CUT AND CHOP

Flourishing is shown here as a training technique to reinforce the use of the cut and chop angles of attack.

The angles of attack were used as early as the Middle Ages. Throughout the European continent into the 1700s and 1800s, we see their application in the form of large wall charts that showed the angles and linked them into a drill sequence for technique retention. In 1821 an English swordsman by the name of Matheson referred to this drill as *flourishing*. The term is also mentioned in some first-person accounts of actual fighting with knife and sword. For this book, I have adapted this concept to portray and retain the angles of attack for the tomahawk executing both cut and chop techniques. I borrowed this approach from the saber and sword manuals from the 1700s and 1800s. The accompanying illustration is from the user's point of view when looking at an anatomical depiction of an opponent. Note the angles and the target areas covered.

## WALL CHART DEPICTING THE ANGLES OF ATTACK FOR FLOURISHING

# EXECUTING THE EIGHT-ANGLE CUT AND CHOP FLOURISHING DRILL

**Training Task:** Execute an eight-angle cut and chop flourishing drill.

**Training Condition:** You are given a wall chart depicting the eight cut and chop angles arrayed on an anatomical silhouette, a wooden or aluminum training knife, and sufficient horizontal and vertical space to conduct the drill safely.

**Training Standard:** Execute at least five repetitions of the complete eight-angle cut and chop flourishing drill a minimum of 3 days a week.

Angle 2          Angle 1

1. Begin with the tomahawk in either a left- or right-side carry. Draw the tomahawk and come to an immediate high guard. Immediately execute an angle 1 cut to the left side of the opponent's head or neck. As the tomahawk passes through the target area, roll the wrist up and effect an angle 2 cut to the right side of the opponent's head or neck. The accompanying illustration depicts this figure-eight action.

43

2. This illustration depicts the first figure-eight pattern of the flourishing drill and the approximate target areas that angles 1 and 2 are directed at. It is shown from the viewpoint of the user.

Angle 3

Angle 4

3. As angle 2 passes through the target area, rotate the palm up, while dropping the tomahawk head toward the ground. Immediately pull the tomahawk upward and across the opponent's left thigh and abdomen area. This completes angle 3.

4. On completion of angle 3, drop the tomahawk head to the left and pull the tomahawk upward and across the opponent's right thigh and abdomen area. This completes angle 4 and the second figure-eight pattern of the flourishing drill.

5. This drawing depicts the second figure-eight pattern of the flourishing drill and the approximate target areas that angles 3 and 4 are directed at. This drawing is from the viewpoint of the user. **NOTE:** Angles 1 through 4 are performed as cuts that flow smoothly through the target areas.

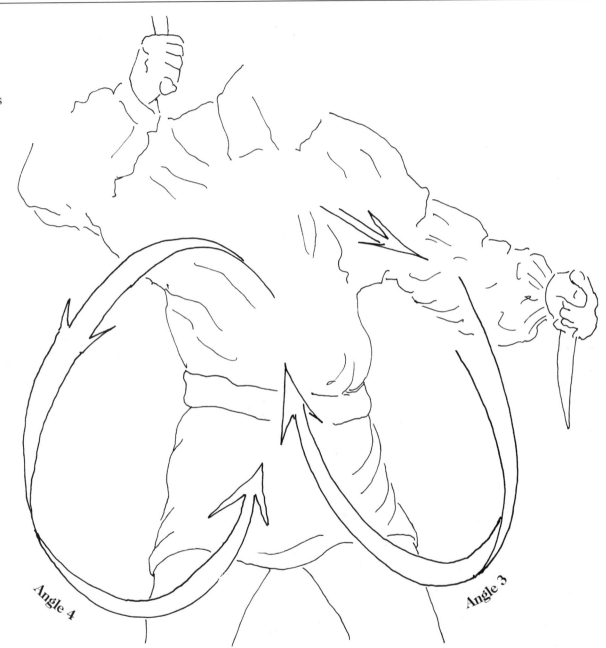

Angle 4

Angle 3

Angle 5

Angle 6

6. On completion of angle 4, retract the tomahawk into a full chamber and then execute a direct chop to the opponent's left rib section, abdomen, or hip. This is angle 5. Again, retract the tomahawk to the left and execute another direct chop to the opponent's right rib section, abdomen, or hip. This is angle 6. **NOTE:** Angles 5 and 6 are chops, which penetrate into the target area. These are not accomplished with the smooth-flowing motion of the cut; rather, they are violent strike-and-retract actions.

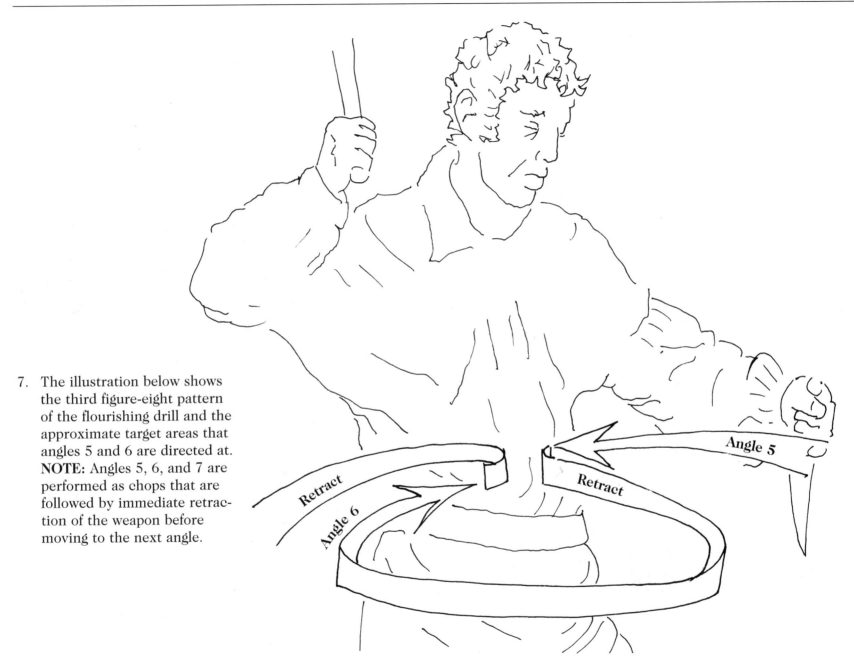

7.  The illustration below shows the third figure-eight pattern of the flourishing drill and the approximate target areas that angles 5 and 6 are directed at. **NOTE:** Angles 5, 6, and 7 are performed as chops that are followed by immediate retraction of the weapon before moving to the next angle.

Angle 7

Angle 8

8. On its retraction from angle 6, turn the head of the tomahawk to the left rear. Then swing the tomahawk in an
upward arc to chop into the opponent's groin or leg area.
This is angle 7. Immediately retract the tomahawk and
swing it in a reverse arc overhead, delivering a final cut to
the opponent's head or face. This is angle 8.

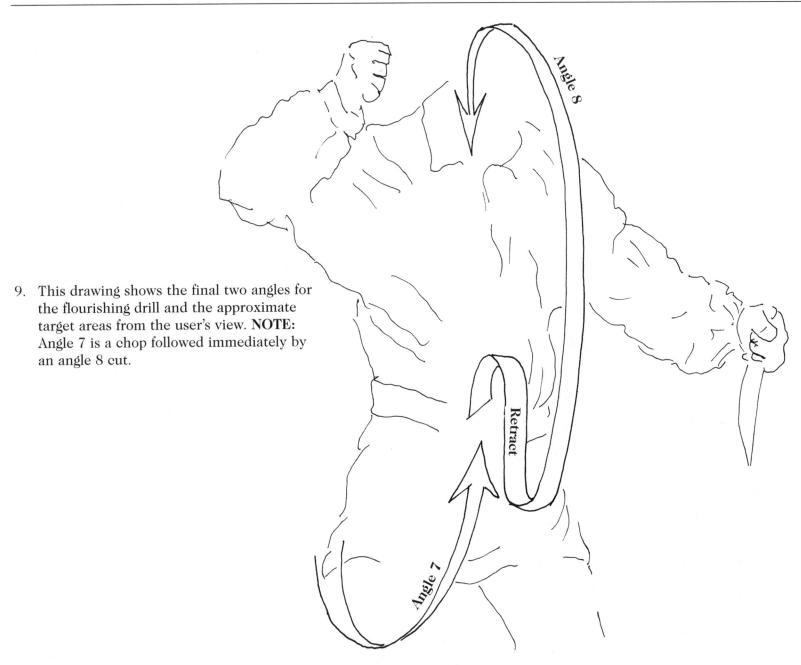

9.  This drawing shows the final two angles for the flourishing drill and the approximate target areas from the user's view. **NOTE:** Angle 7 is a chop followed immediately by an angle 8 cut.

## TRAINING POINTS FOR THE FLOURISHING DRILL

1. Repetitions of this drill should be done very slowly at first. Focus should be on executing both the cut and chop techniques properly. The speed of the drill should be increased gradually. It is strongly recommend that this drill be practiced initially on a wall chart before progressing to a mirror.

2. Once you have attained control with the flourishing drill in the open air and using the wall chart, it is time to progress to the pell, or war post. The pell is usually a log about 12 inches in diameter and approximately 10 feet in length, with 3 feet of the pell buried in the ground. The pell has been used to teach the application of full-force strikes as far back as classical times. The classical Roman scholar Flavius Vegetius' explanation of the use of the pell is as valid today as it was then.

*Similarly, they gave recruits wooden foils, and [of] double weight, instead of swords. Next they were trained at the stakes not only in the morning but also in the afternoon [f]or the use of the*

## TRAINING WITH A WALL CHART

*stakes is greatly advantageous not only for soldiers but also for gladiators. Neither the arena nor the field of battle ever proved a man invincible in arms, except those who are carefully taught training at the stake. However, single stakes ought to be fastened in the ground by individual recruits in such a way that they cannot wobble and they protrude for six feet.*

*The recruit practiced against this stake, just as if against an enemy, with that wicker shield and foil as though with a sword and shield, so that he might aim as if for the head or face. Now he is threatened from the sides, sometimes he endeavors to cut down the hams and shins; he retreats, attacks, leaps in, as if the enemy were present; he assails the stake with all his might, fighting with all skill. In doing this, care was taken that the recruit should strike in this way in order to cause a wound, in case he partly lays himself open to a blow.*

1. **Training Progression:** Training on the pell should be approached slowly at first until you adjust to the impact of full-force strikes. Remember, the point here is to learn to deliver accurate, forceful strikes at speed. Initially practice with each angle singly until you are comfortable with the application. Then begin to execute each of the figure-eight patterns of the flourishing drill. Pay particular attention to the accuracy of the tomahawk head, making sure that you hit what you are aiming at. Finally, execute the entire flourishing drill on the pell.

2. **Attitude and Visualization:** All angles of the flourishing drill should be practiced with the same aggression and resolve that would be used against an actual opponent. Focus should be deliberate, dealing only with the work at hand. There should be no small talk in the vicinity of the exercise. Mental concentration of both students and observers should be totally on the process at hand. As you execute the drill you may use visualization techniques to imagine an opponent using both offensive and defensive tactics against you.

3. **Including the Tomahawk Draw:** When you consider the limited reliability of 18th- and 19th-century flintlock firearms, it is easy to see the need for rapid employment of these backup weapons. All exercises should begin by drawing the tomahawk as part of the drill. Putting the tomahawk and long knife into action rapidly is a skill that requires regular practice to maintain and should be included as part of all exercises contained in this book. As Alexander Withers put it in 1785:

> *[I]n a piece of bottom land in which were no trees, when the Indian turning quickly about with loaded gun uplifted, Hughes' gun was empty, & no tree to spring behind. But instantly springing obliquely to the right and left with bound & outstretched arm, [he] flirted the muzzle of the Indian's gun one side and the next moment had his long knife in him up to the hilt.*

## TRAINING WEAPONS AND WORK ON THE PELL

The ultimate goal of any weapons training is to acquire enough skill to perform all exercises with a fully functional sharp-steel weapon. This is commonly referred to as "live-steel" training. Common sense and sound judgment teach us that live-steel practice is limited to the pell or other targets designed to take the abuse of cutting. Under no circumstances should live steel be used when practicing techniques with a partner.

In today's market there are many expensive custom-forged tomahawks that can be used for work on the pell. However, you must weigh the cost of the weapon against your level of skill to determine if you want to risk damaging the weapon. The best quality forged tomahawk edge can be chipped or bent by a poorly directed cut. It is generally recommended that you use an inexpensive cast tomahawk for live-steel pell practice until you have mastered the requisite skills. Generally, most hardwood tomahawk trainers are not suited to pell work. Those that are constructed in the manner of a live-steel tomahawk do not possess the structural strength for extensive use over a long period. If you do choose to use a wooden tomahawk trainer on the pell, I recommend that you wrap a 1/2-inch fiber rope around the pell to absorb some of the force, reduce damage of wood-on-wood impact, and extend the life of the training weapon.

Hardwood Indian war clubs can be used for pell work. As shown in a later chapter, the war club is used much like the tomahawk and is a good substitute as a high-impact trainer. A war club made from good hardwood will absorb considerable punishment without splintering or cracking.

**Working with a war club
on a rope-wrapped pell**

## TRAINING WEAPONS

There are many commercial knife trainers available, but to date good tomahawk trainers are rare. Most simply do not provide the weight and balance of the real weapon. Some aluminum axes are available and are fine for solo and reenactment purposes, but they are generally much too light for building muscle strength for the real tomahawk. A last option for a tomahawk trainer is to purchase an inexpensive cast tomahawk and grind the edges off until it is smooth and round. These are reasonably safe to use with a training partner, providing that you take the weight of the weapon into account and "pull" blows to make contact light.

Probably the safest method is to pad the edge with leather or cover the head with a sheath, as shown below. This sheath was constructed from 1/4-inch cowhide with an additional 1/4 inch folded over the edge. It slips down over the tomahawk head, where it is laced up from beneath and tied off to the handle. A padded leather cup covers the hammer poll and is laced to the sheath covering the beak.

**Padded leather safety sheath over the toma-hawk head for training**

# Chapter 9

# THE PUNCH

*And at every station [we] would spend an hour
or two in the exercise of tomahawk and rifle, not
only for our own improvement in the use of these
weapons of warfare but also to alarm the savages if
they should be lurking in the neighborhood.*
—John Struthers, 1777 (excerpted from Mark
Baker's *The Sons of the Trackless Forest*)

The punch is delivered in a manner very similar to the thrust that is used with knives and swords. Historically, some war axes had a spike on the tip to facilitate use in thrusting or punching. Some head designs (see right) extend the edge beyond the tip, which also can produce deep puncture wounds. The tomahawk, or trade ax, we are working with does not have this capability; however, the head can produce a devastating impact wound when using the same technique.

For speed of delivery and rapid engagement potential, the punch is superior to the cut or chop; it simply provides the shortest distance to the target. The punch is best delivered from a middle-guard position, with arms extended or in full chamber with either the hammer or extended grip. The long, full-choke, or half-choke position may be applied, depending on the combat range.

The punch is particularly effective in gaining time against an onrushing opponent. In this situation the head or throat is usually the target. The punch is shown on the following two pages.

### AXES WITH THRUSTING AND PUNCHING CAPABILITY

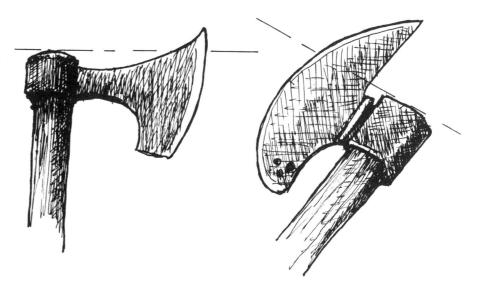

## VISUALIZATION OF THE PUNCH

## ANATOMY OF A TOMAHAWK PUNCH

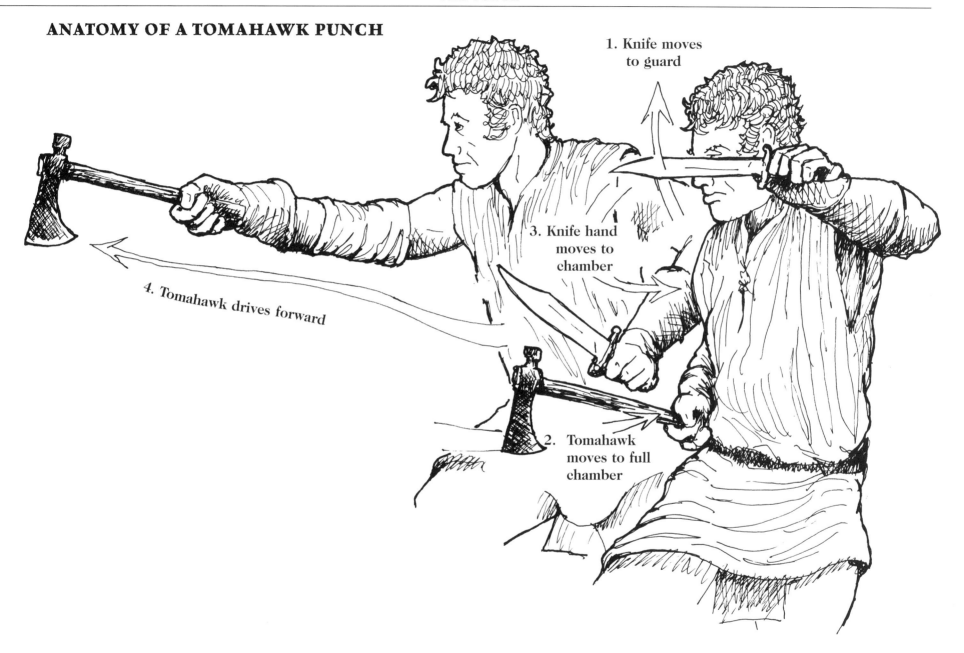

1. Knife moves to guard

3. Knife hand moves to chamber

4. Tomahawk drives forward

2. Tomahawk moves to full chamber

# THE NINE-ANGLE PUNCH DRILL

The sequence depicted on the following pages is designed to reinforce the punch at high-, mid-, and lowline targets. The drill consists of three punches to an opponent's head (punches 1–3), three punches to an opponent's midsection (punches 4–6), and three punches to an opponent's legs and groin (punches 7–9). These areas, shown here and on the following page, will be referred to throughout this book.

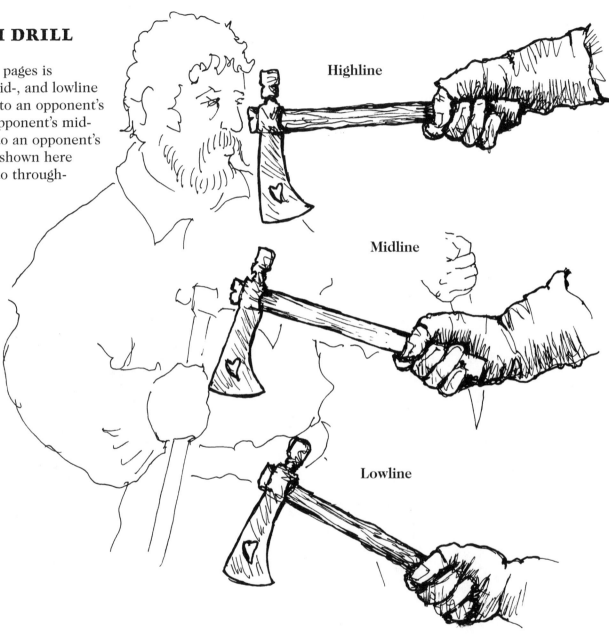

Highline

Midline

Lowline

## PRESENTING THE TOMAHAWK HEAD DURING A PUNCH

Along each attack line (high, mid, and low), the tomahawk head may be rotated left or right to present the widest area of the head. This increases the accuracy and efficiency of the strike.

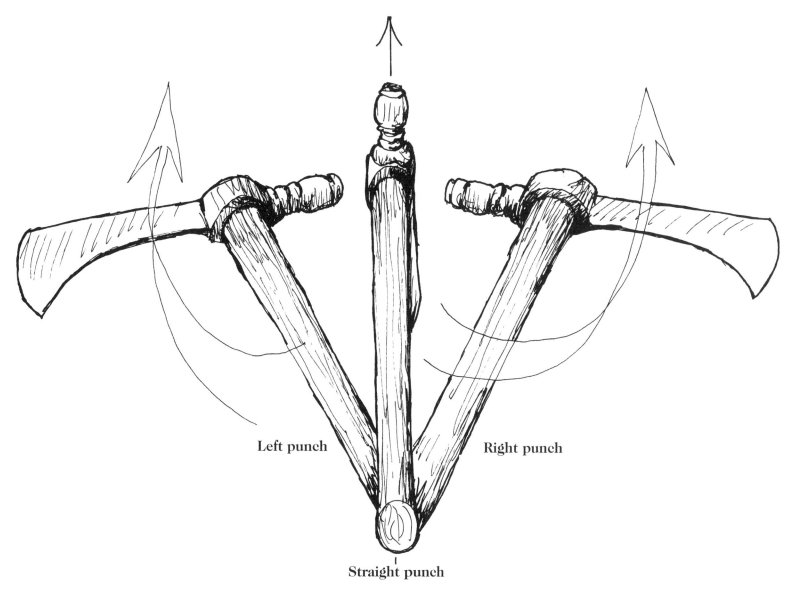

Left punch

Right punch

Straight punch

## EXECUTING THE NINE-ANGLE PUNCH DRILL

**Training Task:** Execute the nine-angle punch in a progressive sequence.

**Training Condition:** You are given an anatomical silhouette wall chart or mirror, a wooden or aluminum training tomahawk, and sufficient horizontal and vertical space to perform the drill safely.

**Training Standard:** Execute a complete nine-angle punch drill a minimum of five repetitions 3 days a week.

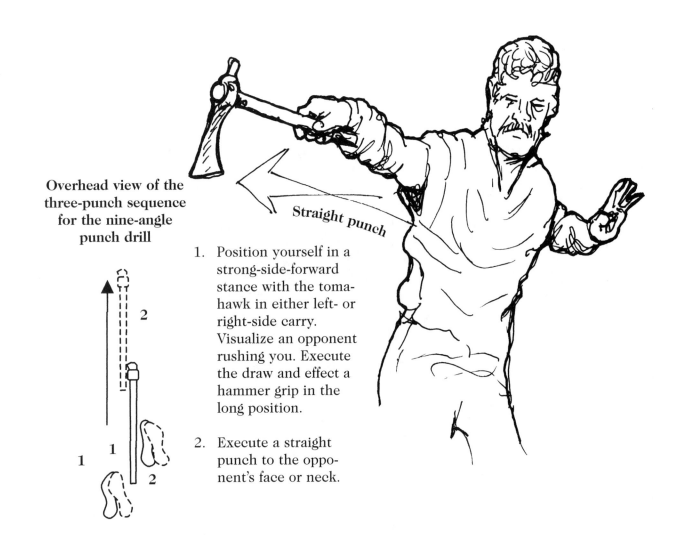

Overhead view of the three-punch sequence for the nine-angle punch drill

Straight punch

1. Position yourself in a strong-side-forward stance with the tomahawk in either left- or right-side carry. Visualize an opponent rushing you. Execute the draw and effect a hammer grip in the long position.

2. Execute a straight punch to the opponent's face or neck.

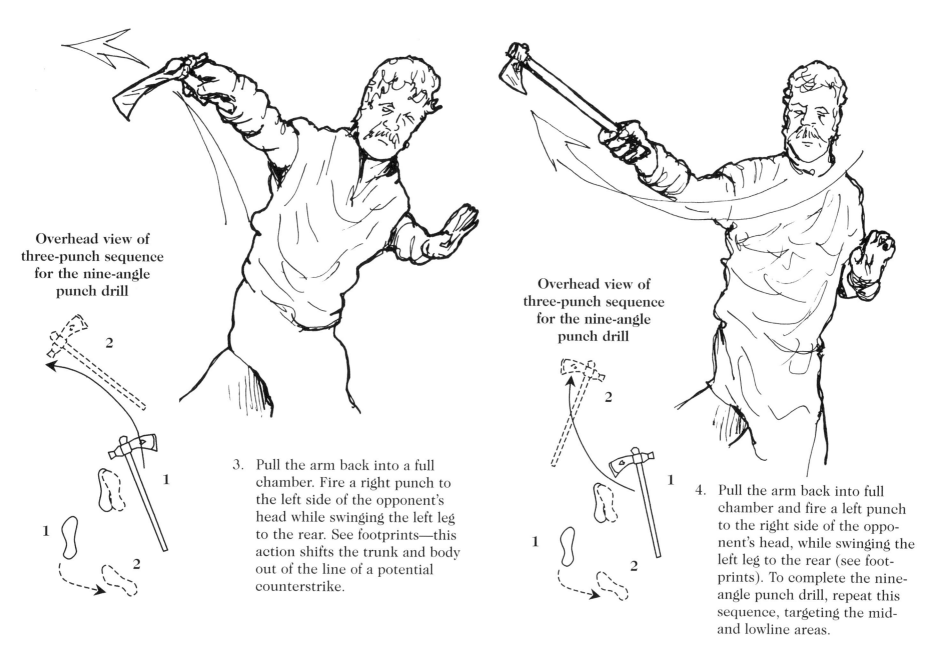

**Overhead view of three-punch sequence for the nine-angle punch drill**

3. Pull the arm back into a full chamber. Fire a right punch to the left side of the opponent's head while swinging the left leg to the rear. See footprints—this action shifts the trunk and body out of the line of a potential counterstrike.

**Overhead view of three-punch sequence for the nine-angle punch drill**

4. Pull the arm back into full chamber and fire a left punch to the right side of the opponent's head, while swinging the left leg to the rear (see footprints). To complete the nine-angle punch drill, repeat this sequence, targeting the mid- and lowline areas.

## EFFECTIVE PUNCH TARGETS

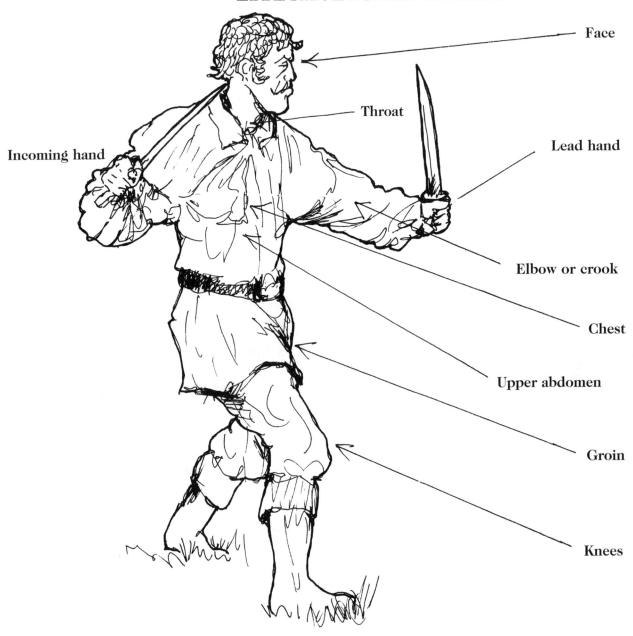

Face

Throat

Incoming hand

Lead hand

Elbow or crook

Chest

Upper abdomen

Groin

Knees

# Chapter 10

# THE RAKE

*[F]or a while forgot that his gun was yet charged. The recollection of this, inspiring him with fresh hopes, he wheeled to fire at his pursuer, but found him so close that he could not bring his gun to bear on him. Having greatly the advantage of ground, he thrust him back with his hand.*
—Alexander Withers, from a 1777 account

Many 18th-century accounts of fights indicate that after an initial discharge of musket fire, the Indians often attempted to rapidly close with their opponent. Sometimes this was preceded by throwing the tomahawk and then rushing in with the knife before the opponent could employ his sidearms. Earlier we discussed the use of the hammer grip in the full-choke position. This is usually the position that the hand is in when initiating a tomahawk draw from a right- or left-carry position. Imagine yourself at this stage of a draw with the opponent within arm's reach and closing. There is no time to execute any of the hand shifts described earlier—the enemy is upon you! The tomahawk must be employed in close quarters with the full choke.

This technique, used with the full choke at such close range, is the rake. The following pages illustrate the rake technique.

## APPLICATION OF THE RAKE

At close quarters, the rake is applied with a circular motion of the wrist, with approximately 1 inch of the edge and spine (point) of the beak, to produce a jagged wound that results in considerable shock to the opponent. This is especially effective when used against the ribs, groin, or throat. Note in the drawing below that a penetration of about 1 inch is usual.

## ANATOMY OF A HORIZONTAL RAKE, RIGHT TO LEFT

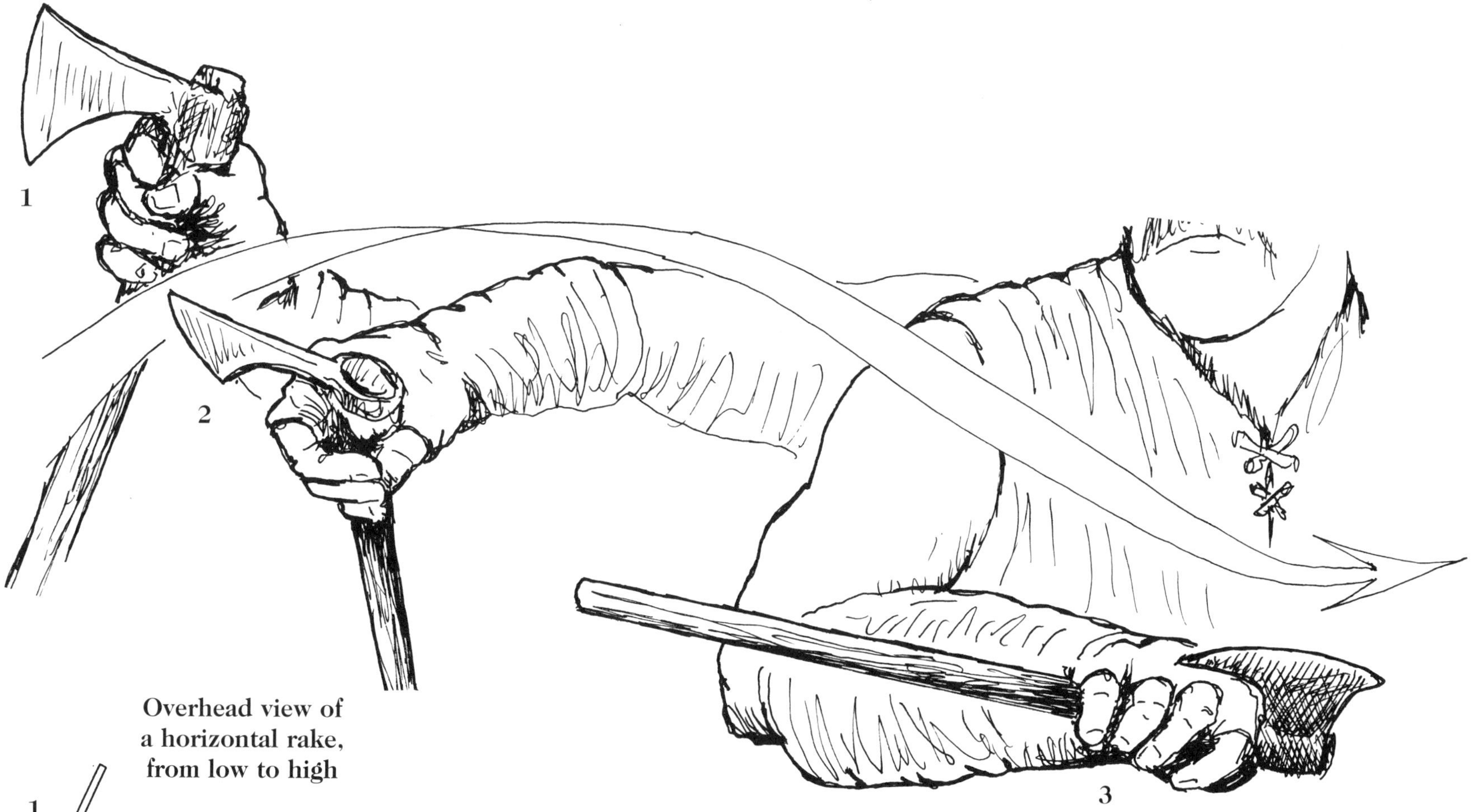

1

2

Overhead view of
a horizontal rake,
from low to high

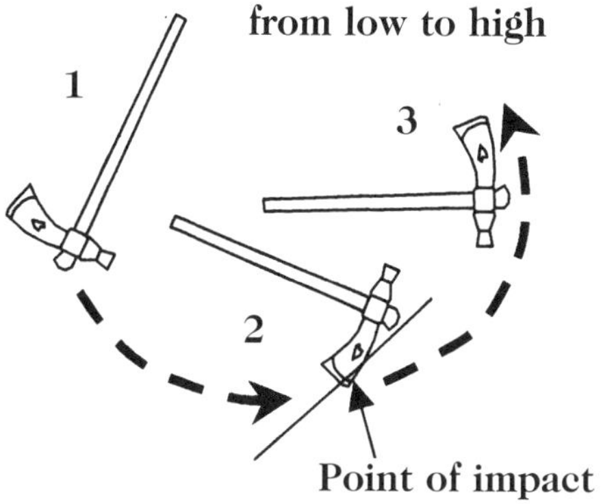

1

3

2

Point of impact

3

## ANATOMY OF A HORIZONTAL RAKE, LEFT TO RIGHT

Overhead view of horizontal rake from left to right

Point of impact

## ANATOMY OF A VERTICAL RAKE, HIGH TO LOW

View of vertical rake
from high to low

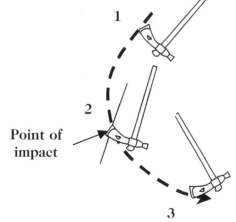

Point of
impact

## ANATOMY OF A VERTICAL RAKE, LOW TO HIGH

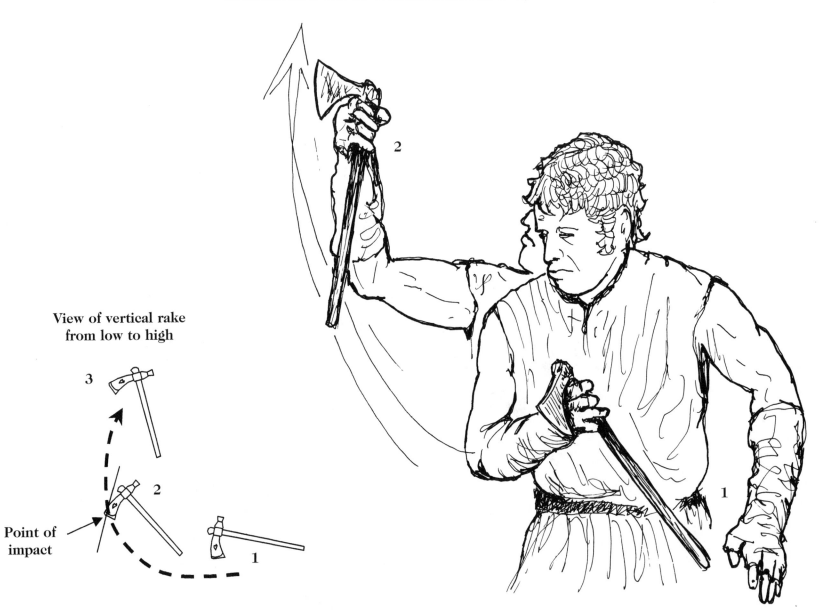

View of vertical rake
from low to high

3

2

1

Point of
impact

# FOUR-ANGLE DRILL TO
# REINFORCE THE USE OF THE RAKE

The drill sequence depicted on the following pages is composed of four major angles of attack and is used in a manner similar to the flourishing drill, except that the motion between angles of attack is not smooth or flowing. Rather, each angle is performed in an abrupt, circular, whipping action.

**Training Task:** Execute the four-angle rake drill in a progressive sequence.

**Training Condition:** You are given an anatomical silhouette wall chart or mirror, a wooden or aluminum training tomahawk, and sufficient horizontal and vertical space to conduct the drill safely.

**Training Standard:** Execute the complete four-angle rake drill a minimum of five repetitions 3 days a week.

## Executing the Four-Angle Rake Drill

1. Position yourself in a strong-side-forward stance with the tomahawk in a left-side-carry position. Visualize the opponent rushing you. Pass your right hand quickly across the abdomen, securing a palm-up full-choke hammer grip.

2. As the tomahawk is pulled free of the belt, violently drive it upward in a short arc toward the opponent's midsection. **NOTE:** The initial impact can be directed to the groin, abdomen, chest, throat, or chin. If the intent is to double the opponent over, a strike to the groin or abdomen will produce that result. If you wish to push the opponent backward, then attack the throat or chin.

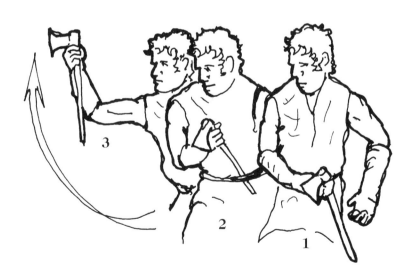

3.  Immediately rotate the wrist about 180 degrees to point the tomahawk's head toward the ground. Violently pull the point of the head vertically through the opponent's face, continuing this descent through the chest and abdomen.

4.  Rotate the tomahawk approximately 180 degrees to the right, and with a circular, whipping action drag the head across the opponent's arm or chest area.

5.  As the tomahawk head clears the opponent's left arm, rotate the head approximately 180 degrees to the left and execute a circular, whipping action to drag the tomahawk across the arm and chest area.

## WALL CHART FOR FOUR-ANGLE RAKE DRILL

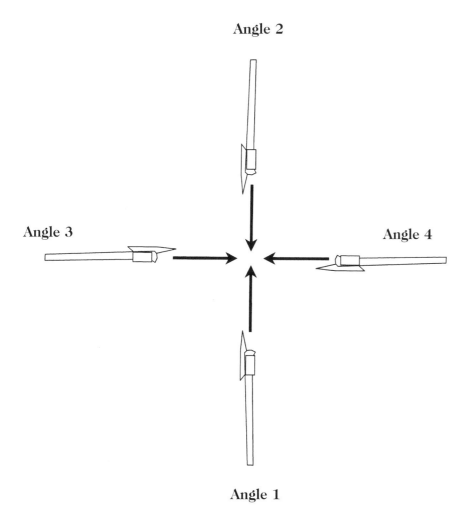

Angle 2

Angle 3

Angle 4

Angle 1

## TRAINING POINTS FOR USE WITH THE FOUR-ANGLE RAKE

1. **Training Progression:** Repetitions of this drill should be done slowly until the technical aspects of the rake are mastered. Remember that this is not a flowing exercise but a series of circular, whipping actions designed to disrupt and damage muscle tissue and tear ligaments. This is a violent action drill.

2. **Pell Training:** This is essential to achieving accuracy with the rake. Gloves or hand protection is necessary because of the possibility of jamming the hand against the tomahawk head.

3. **Attitude and Visualization:** Practice all rake exercises as if against an opponent who has advanced rapidly on you. You are locked in close-quarter combat, and for all purposes you are in the clutches of a more powerful enemy. You must use the rake techniques to break free and create openings to attack.

4. **Including the Tomahawk Draw:** All exercises should begin with the draw. The situation is that the opponent has grabbed you before completing the draw and you are in a full-choke hammer grip. Remember that angle 1 of the drill is executed directly from the draw.

# PART III

## Defensive Use of the Tomahawk

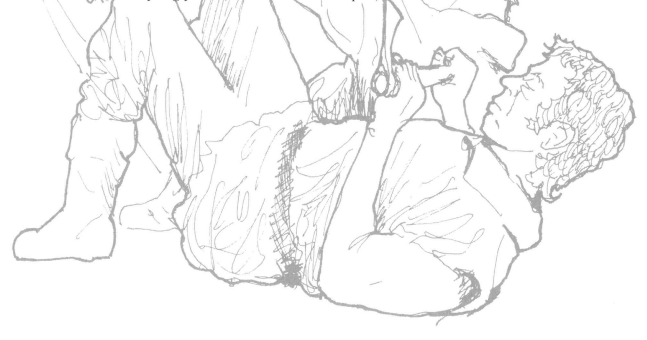

**T**he tomahawk is first and foremost an offensive weapon, but it can be used defensively. The techniques in Part III should be viewed as protective action to avoid an attack while simultaneously creating an opening for a counterattack. For our purposes there are four defensive techniques: the deflection, intercepting punch, circular catch and pull, and two-handed block.

# Chapter 11

# THE DEFLECTION

T he deflection as applied to the tomahawk is very similar to the technique used with a large knife or a sword in parrying an opponent's attack to create an opening. This is normally a smooth-flowing action that relies on a simple rotation of the wrist or hand to take an opponent's incoming attack off the line of his intended target. Usually this action creates an opening for the delivery of a counterattack. The tomahawk does not have enough edge surface to accomplish this; therefore, the action involves a more violent deflection strike to set up delivery of a counter cut or chop. The mechanics of the deflection are abrupt and do not flow as smoothly as a parry with a sword, saber, or long knife.

There are basically two types of deflections. The first involves impact with the hammer or base of the tomahawk head. The second uses either the edge or flat of the beak to deflect a strike. For lack of specific terms, I call these *base deflection* and *edge deflection* (sometimes referred to as *beak deflection*).

**Action 1:** An opponent delivers an angle 2 strike to your head as you move through the middle-guard position. Abruptly pull the tomahawk head backward in an arc to intercept the incoming weapon. Note that the edge and beak of the tomahawk are trailing.

**Action 2:** The opponent's weapon is deflected, leaving an opening.

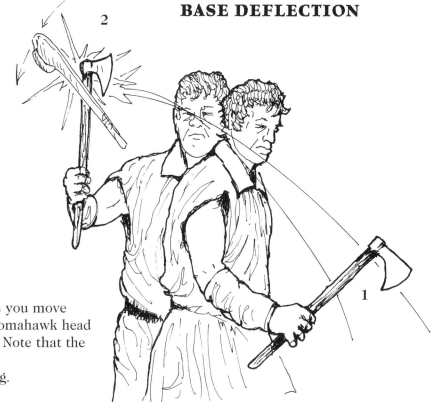

**BASE DEFLECTION**

## CLOSE-UP OF BASE DEFLECTION

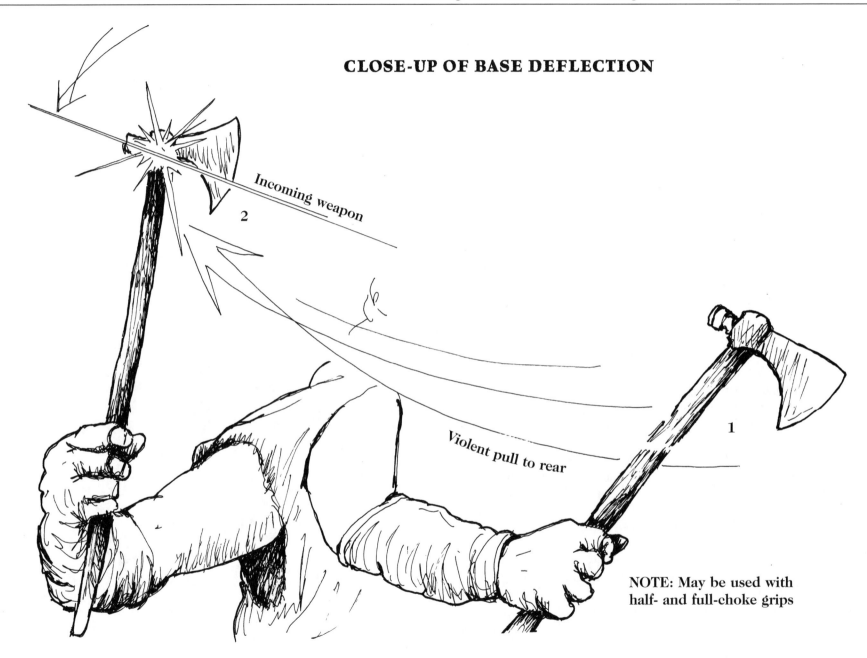

Incoming weapon

2

Violent pull to rear

1

NOTE: May be used with
half- and full-choke grips

## BASE DEFLECTION AGAINST MIDLINE ATTACK

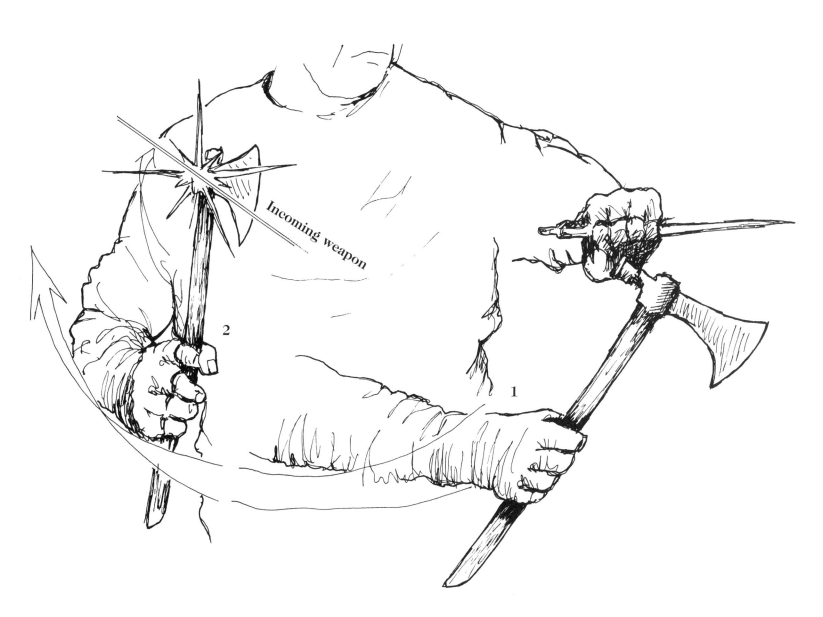

Incoming weapon

## BASE DEFLECTION AGAINST SIX ATTACK ANGLES (DEFENDER'S VIEW)

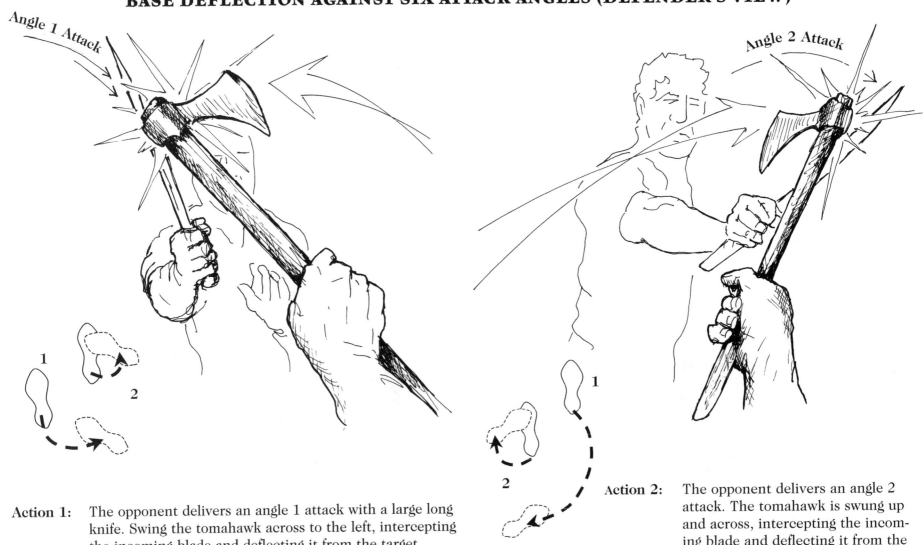

**Action 1:** The opponent delivers an angle 1 attack with a large long knife. Swing the tomahawk across to the left, intercepting the incoming blade and deflecting it from the target. Simultaneously swing the left foot to the rear and pivot the right foot to the right. This moves the head and torso off the target line, facilitating a smoother deflection and revealing openings to counterattack (see footprints).

**Action 2:** The opponent delivers an angle 2 attack. The tomahawk is swung up and across, intercepting the incoming blade and deflecting it from the target to the right. Simultaneously, the right foot is swung to the rear, and the left foot is pivoted to the left, moving off the target line.

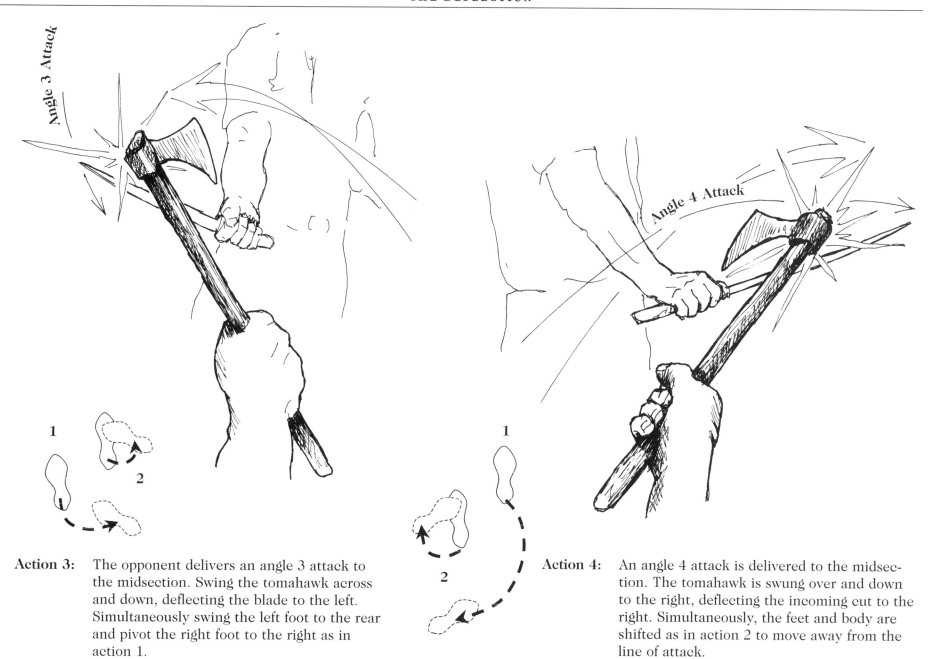

**Action 3:** The opponent delivers an angle 3 attack to the midsection. Swing the tomahawk across and down, deflecting the blade to the left. Simultaneously swing the left foot to the rear and pivot the right foot to the right as in action 1.

**Action 4:** An angle 4 attack is delivered to the midsection. The tomahawk is swung over and down to the right, deflecting the incoming cut to the right. Simultaneously, the feet and body are shifted as in action 2 to move away from the line of attack.

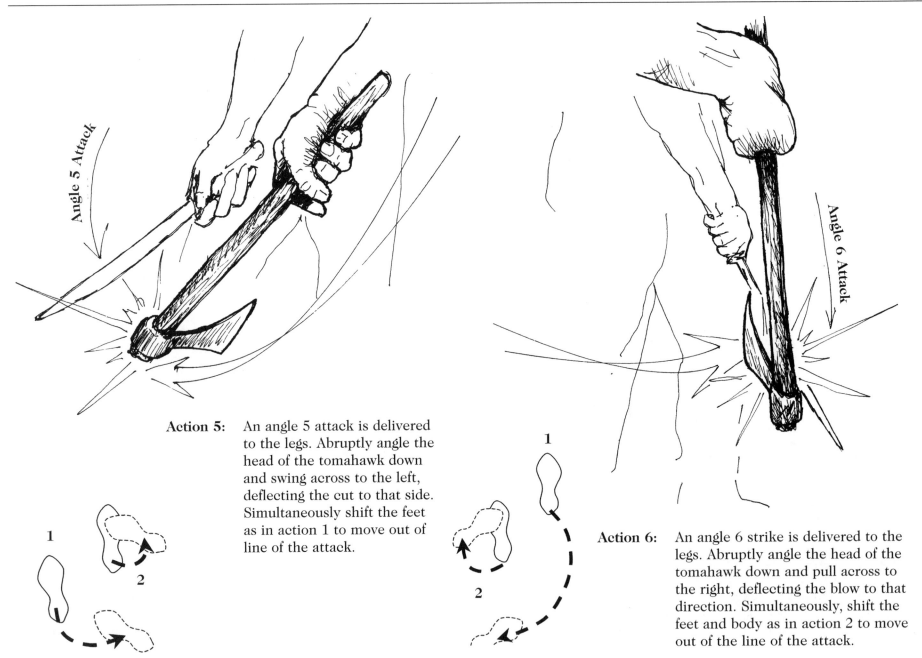

Angle 5 Attack

Angle 6 Attack

**Action 5:** An angle 5 attack is delivered to the legs. Abruptly angle the head of the tomahawk down and swing across to the left, deflecting the cut to that side. Simultaneously shift the feet as in action 1 to move out of line of the attack.

**Action 6:** An angle 6 strike is delivered to the legs. Abruptly angle the head of the tomahawk down and pull across to the right, deflecting the blow to that direction. Simultaneously, shift the feet and body as in action 2 to move out of the line of the attack.

# WALL CHART FOR THE BASE DEFLECTION DRILL AGAINST SIX ATTACK ANGLES

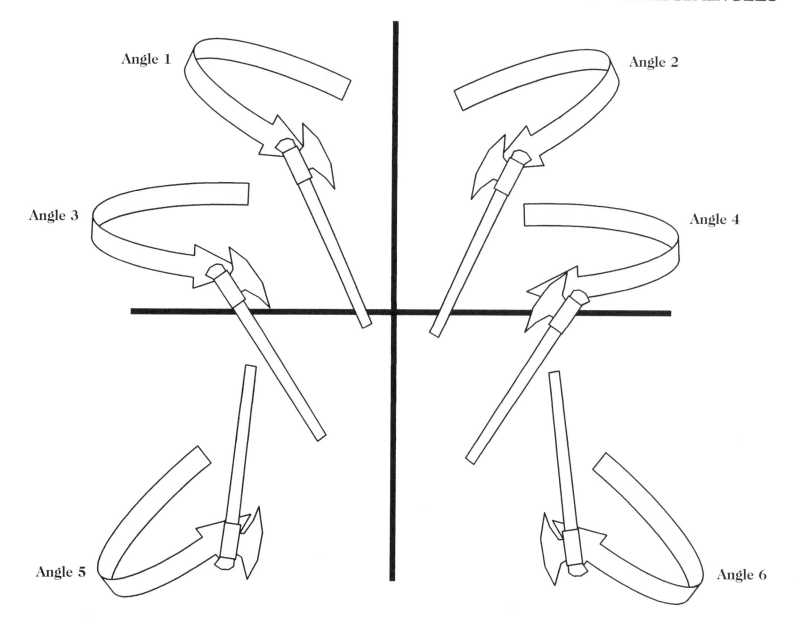

## BASE-DEFLECTION TECHNIQUES

**1. Training Progression**

    a. The solo base deflection drill consists of six actions. Along with the foot movement, these actions should be practiced sequentially with one action flowing smoothly into another. These can be done standing in front of a mirror or using the wall chart.

    b. The base-deflection drill can be practiced with a training partner who delivers the six angles of attack. Both partners should face each other at a range where each weapon touches only a few inches. During initial training this drill should be practiced with both partners remaining stationary. The drill begins with the attacker executing an angle 1 attack and continuing through the subsequent six angles sequentially. The defending partner executes action 1 through 6 base deflections to each respective angle. This drill should first be performed slowly until both partners have mastered the method. Once proficiency is attained, the speed can be increased to half speed and ultimately full speed. Begin with the static position and then progress to forward, backward, and circular movements. **SAFETY NOTE:** Never perform these drills without effective head, eye, arm, body, and groin protection, and use only wood, blunted metal, or padded weapons, never live steel.

    c. These training exercises should be practiced in sets of three repetitions of all six base deflections a minimum of three times weekly.

**2. Attitude and Visualization**

    a. Proficiency is achieved by practicing all drills aggressively.

    b. As each deflection is executed, look for or visualize potential openings in the opponent's guard for counterattack.

    c. During all drills, the attacker should take special care to give the defender safe yet accurate and realistic attacks that force him to execute the deflection correctly.

## WALL CHART OF INCOMING ATTACK ANGLES

NOTE: This is used to assist in visualization for base-deflection drills.

## EDGE DEFLECTION

Edge deflection involves impact with the edge or side of the tomahawk. The relatively small size of most tomahawk heads makes this technique difficult to master, and it requires a consistent training regimen to maintain proficiency. Deflections against angles 1 and 2 attack are easier to master than those of the mid- and low-lines. Presenting the edge for impact is awkward and requires passing the legs and acutely twisting the torso. For this reason it is recommended that the edge deflection be used only against highline attacks. Shown here is an edge deflection against a highline attack. **NOTE:** The training progression used for the base-deflection drill may be used for the edge-deflection techniques.

## DELIVERING THE EDGE DEFLECTION

The sequence on the following pages illustrates the edge deflection against six angles of attack.

**Action 1:** An opponent delivers an angle 1 strike to your head. Rotate the wrist to the left while simultaneously pulling the tomahawk across the body. With the edge or side of the tomahawk hit the forward portion of the incoming weapon.

**Action 2:** On impact, pull the tomahawk through and directly into a midline counterattack.

# EDGE-DEFLECTION TECHNIQUES AGAINST SIX ANGLES OF ATTACK

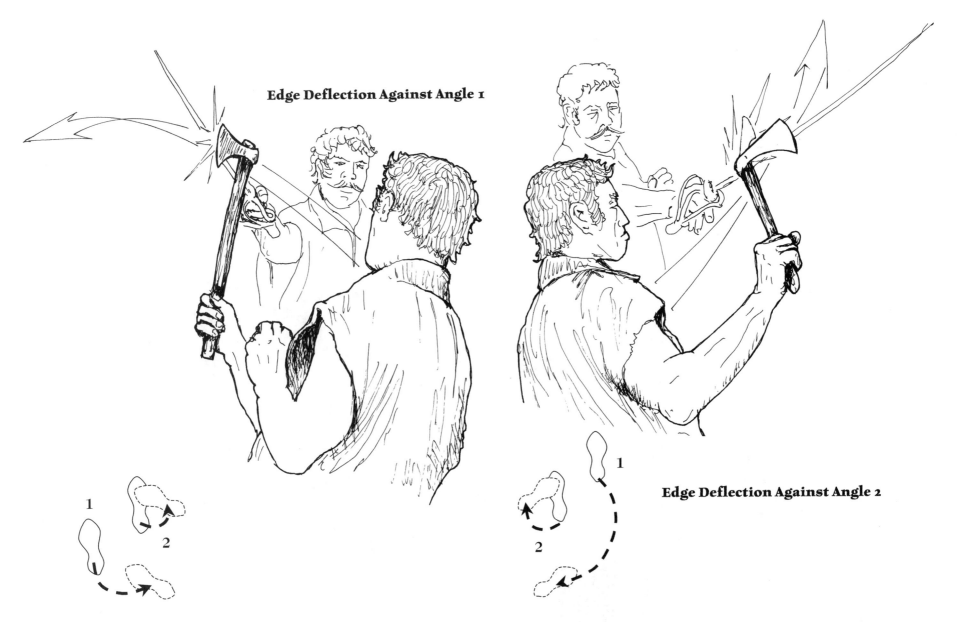

Edge Deflection Against Angle 1

Edge Deflection Against Angle 2

**Edge Deflection Against Angle 3**

**Edge Deflection Against Angle 4**

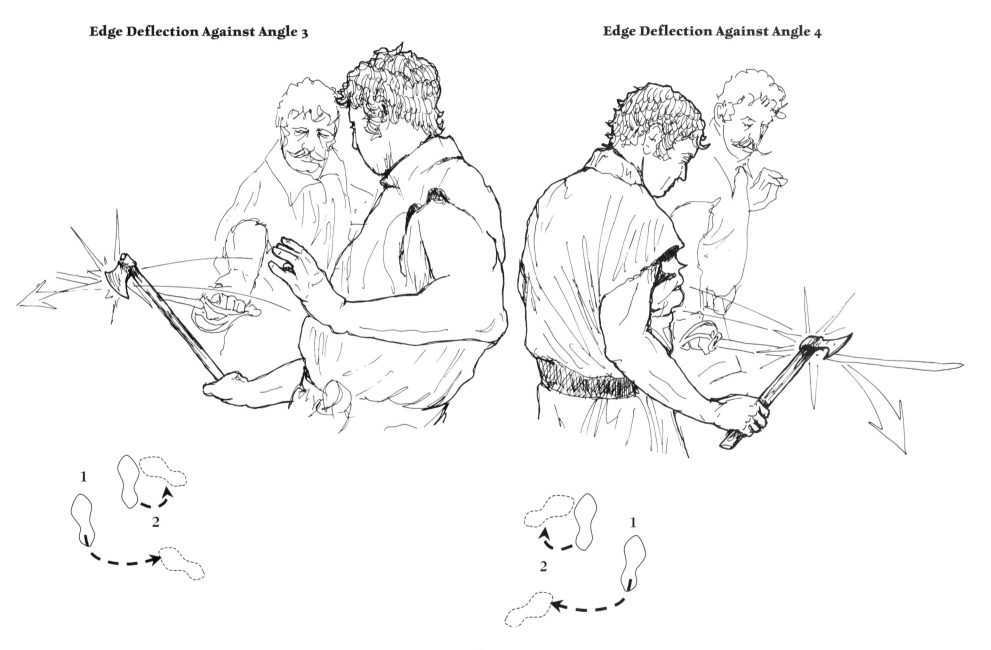

**Edge Deflection Against Angle 5**

**Edge Deflection Against Angle 6**

# Chapter 12

# THE INTERCEPTING PUNCH

**T**he second protective technique is the intercepting punch. It can be used against any of the attacks on the wall chart shown earlier. Punch techniques are very effective in disrupting an attack by intercepting the blow before it achieves momentum. In this case, the punch need not always be directed against the weapon; such targets as the hand, wrist, arm, shoulder, throat, and chin may be hit to deflect the blow.

# VISUALIZATION OF AN INTERCEPTING PUNCH TO AN OPPONENT'S ARM, DISRUPTING AN OVERHEAD STRIKE

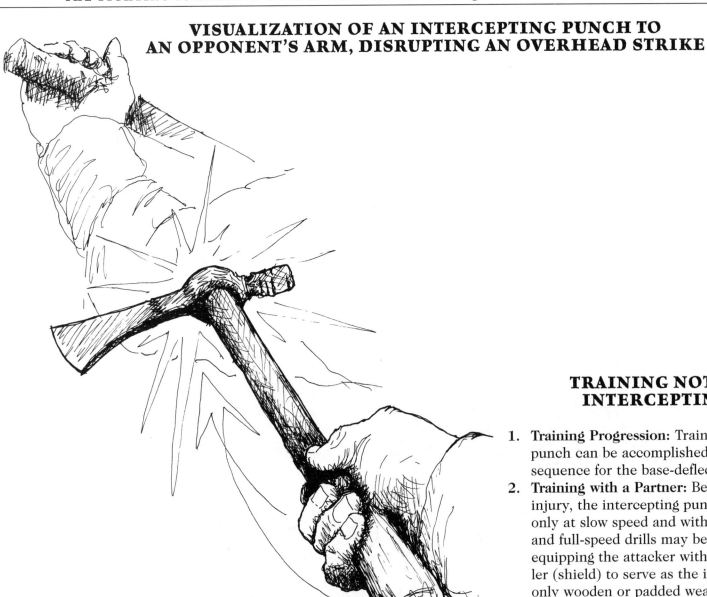

## TRAINING NOTE FOR THE INTERCEPTING PUNCH

1. **Training Progression:** Training for the intercepting punch can be accomplished as a solo drill using the sequence for the base-deflection drill.
2. **Training with a Partner:** Because of the potential for injury, the intercepting punch should be practiced only at slow speed and with padded weapons. Half- and full-speed drills may be performed safely by equipping the attacker with a wooden or leather buckler (shield) to serve as the incoming target. Again, only wooden or padded weapons should be used.

# Chapter 13

# THE CIRCULAR CATCH AND PULL

One of the obvious advantages of any tomahawk or ax is the ease with which the bill can catch an opponent's weapon or limb. The circular catch and pull is usually accomplished by hitting the head or handle on the limb or weapon and immediately dropping the hook portion of the tomahawk beak over (see illustration at right). This action is usually executed simultaneously with a lateral or upward pulling action. Although many cite the great advantages of the catch and pull, it should be used only with a clear understanding of the following principles:

1. The catch and pull is more effective against bladed weapons. When it is executed against another ax-like weapon, the technique can be easily reversed and performed against the executor.

2. When it is performed against an empty hand, the opponent can seize the handle and twist the weapon from the user's grip. The catch-and-pull technique is very effective against the lower leg or ankle and can be used in conjunction with a variety of push and trip techniques to topple the opponent (left).

## ANATOMY OF A CATCH AND PULL

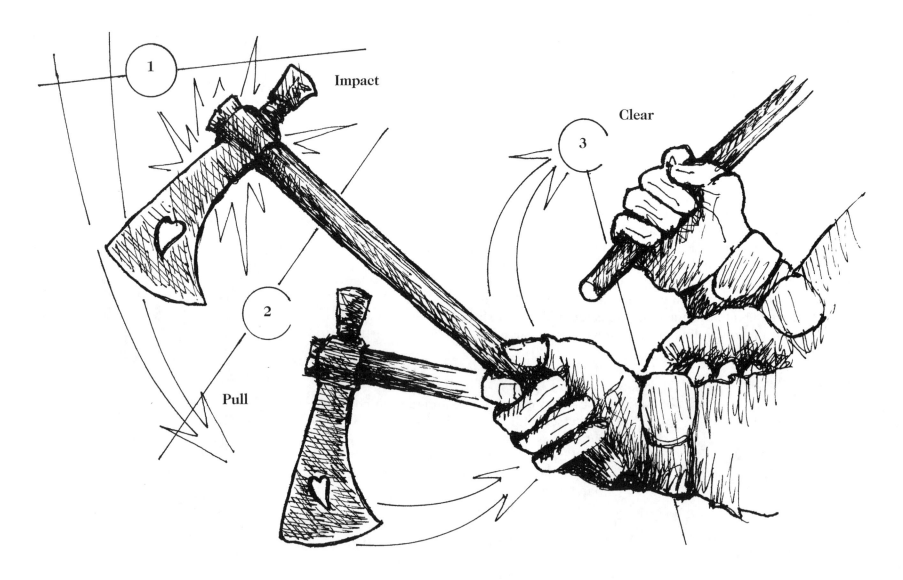

# TRAINING NOTE FOR THE CIRCULAR CATCH-AND-PULL DRILL

One should visualize the catch-and-pull techniques as two half-circles, one to the left side (addresses angles 1, 3, and 5 attacks) and one to the right side (addresses angles 2, 4, and 6 attacks). This pattern runs from high- to lowline on the target area. In other words, the tomahawk descends to effect the catch. The drawing below depicts the aspects of the catch-and-pull technique against six angles of attack.

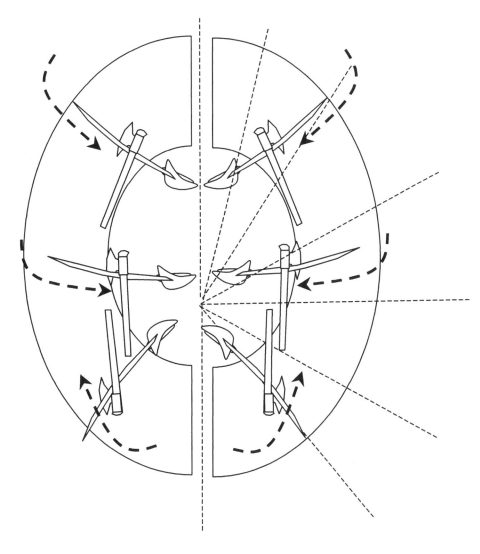

## FRONTAL VIEW OF THE HALF CIRCLES FOR THE CATCH-AND-PULL TECHNIQUE

# EXECUTING THE CATCH-AND-PULL SEQUENCE

**Training Task:** Execute the catch-and-pull drill in a progressive sequence.

**Training Condition:** You are given an anatomical silhouette wall chart or mirror, a wooden or aluminum training tomahawk, and enough horizontal and vertical space to perform the sequence safely.

**Training Standard:** Execute at least five repetitions of the catch-and-pull drill 3 days a week.

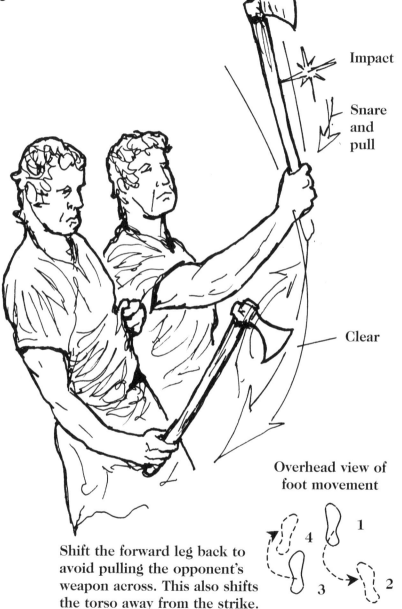

Impact

Snare and pull

Clear

Overhead view of foot movement

Shift the forward leg back to avoid pulling the opponent's weapon across. This also shifts the torso away from the strike.

1. Position yourself in a strong-side-forward stance with the tomahawk in either a left- or right-side carry. Visualize an opponent delivering angle 1 through 6 attacks. Execute the draw to an extended grip in long position.

2. Visualize angle 1 incoming. Intercept, snare, and pull down the opponent's weapon or limb. **IMPORTANT POINT:** In the accompanying illustration the *clearing* action refers to the third action depicted in the illustration of the anatomy of a catch and pull (page 90). Once the opponent's weapon or limb has been moved to the desired position, it is necessary to disengage the tomahawk to put it back into play against the opponent. This clearing action is normally accomplished by pushing the tomahawk's head back in the opposite direction or by twisting the head to either side and continuing to pull across into a full chamber with the arm. Execute a clearing action.

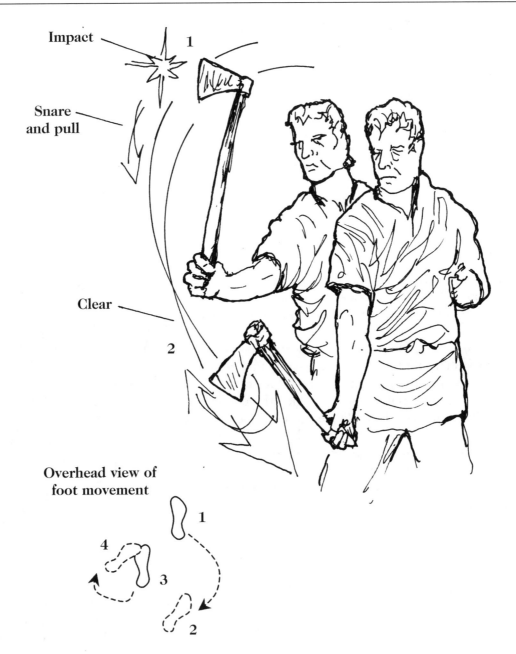

Impact

1

Snare
and pull

3. Visualize an angle 2 incoming.
   Intercept, snare, pull down,
   and clear the opponent's
   weapon or limb.

Clear

2

Overhead view of
foot movement

4

1

3

2

94

4. Visualize an angle 3 coming at your midsection. Intercept, snare, pull down, and clear the opponent's weapon or limb.

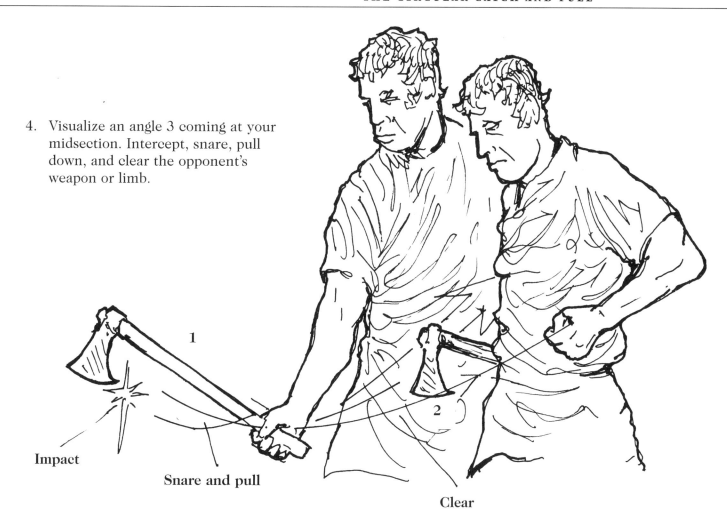

Impact

Snare and pull

Clear

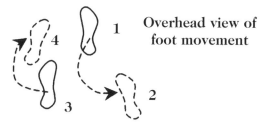

Overhead view of foot movement

5.  Visualize an angle 4 coming at you midsection. Intercept, snare, pull down, and clear the opponent's weapon or limb.

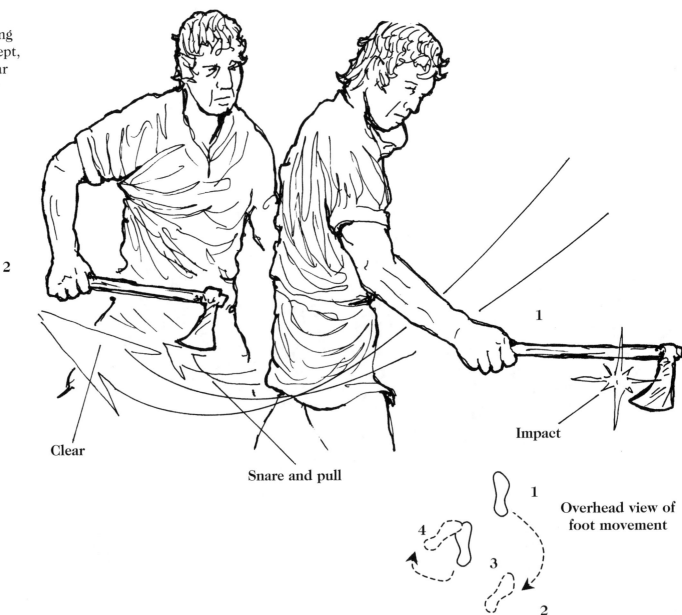

2

1

Clear

Snare and pull

Impact

Overhead view of foot movement

1

4

3

2

6. Visualize an angle 5 coming at your legs. Drop the head of the tomahawk down and to your left. Pull up, impact, snare, and clear.

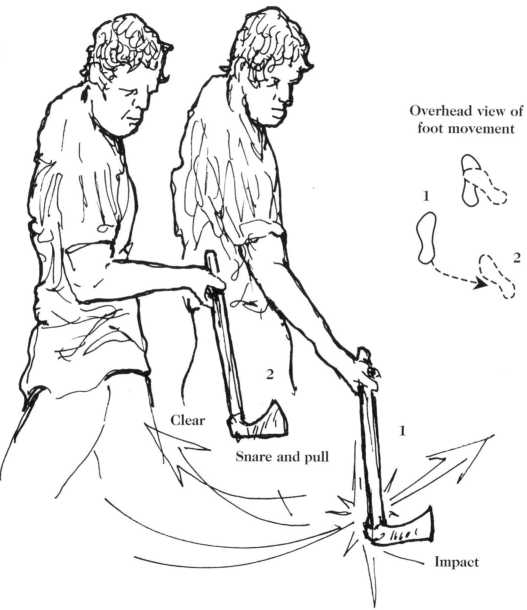

Overhead view of foot movement

1

2

Clear

2

Snare and pull

1

Impact

97

7. Visualize an angle 6 coming at your legs. Drop the tomahawk head down and to the right, impact, snare, pull up, and clear.

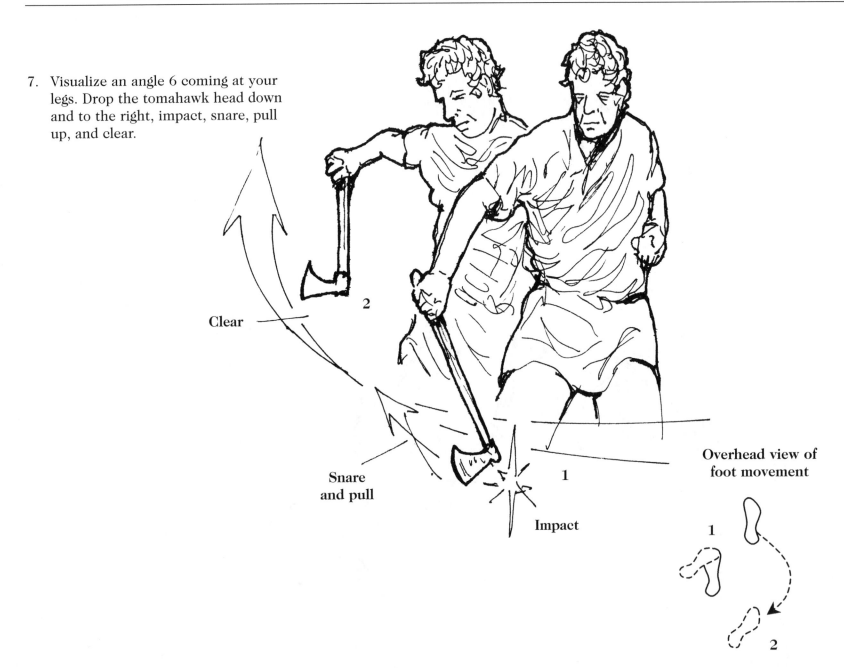

Clear

2

Snare
and pull

Impact

1

Overhead view of
foot movement

1

2

# Chapter 14

# THE TWO-HANDED BLOCK

T he final protection technique is the two-handed block. This is a timeless method that can be traced back through the centuries in the use of the sword, saber, staff, spear, and bayonet. Here I show only the fundamental applications; I'll leave the more detailed aspects of handling and levering for another text.

The two-handed block means gripping the tomahawk with both hands: one at the end of the handle, as in a long grip, and the other next to the head. This can be done with both hands in an overhand grip or in a mixed grip where the hand nearer the head is in the underhand position. This technique is normally used at medium or close range when an opponent's blow takes you by surprise. It is a hasty defense measure that is usually followed up with an immediate counterattack, usually preceded by pushing the opponent's weapon to the left or right to obtain an opening. These blocking measures are used against strikes from the front and horizontal attacks to either side.

A frontal attack may come in as an overhead strike to the head or shoulders or as an uppercut to the mid-thigh and groin areas. Against the overhead strike you drive both arms forcefully upward, hitting the opponent's weapon on the center of the tomahawk handle. Simultaneously, your feet slide forward. Against heavy sabers (or cutlasses) and the ax, the impact should be absorbed midway on the opponent's blade or handle, and the tomahawk handle should be pushed forward to hit the opponent's hands or guard. Against the upward cut, move the nearer threatened leg quickly to the rear, while simultaneously pulling the tomahawk down, striking in a manner similar to the overhead block.

**VISUALIZATION OF FRONTAL BLOCK**

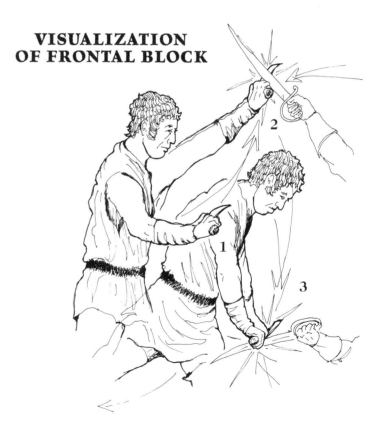

99

## VISUALIZATION OF HORIZONTAL BLOCK

Horizontal blocks against lateral strikes to the midsection are done by dropping either your left or right hand and forcefully pushing the tomahawk handle into the strike. In the illustration below, note that the torso is twisted away from the strike.

Accounts of Indian raids from the 18th century tell of individuals being knocked to the ground and subjected to devastating blows from the war club or tomahawk. One of the advantages of mastering the frontal and horizontal blocks is their applicability to this type of combat situation. Along with these blocks, the downed victim can use his feet and legs to protect himself and deliver kicks to the opponent's legs and groin.

## FRONTAL BLOCK DELIVERED FROM GROUND WITH KICK

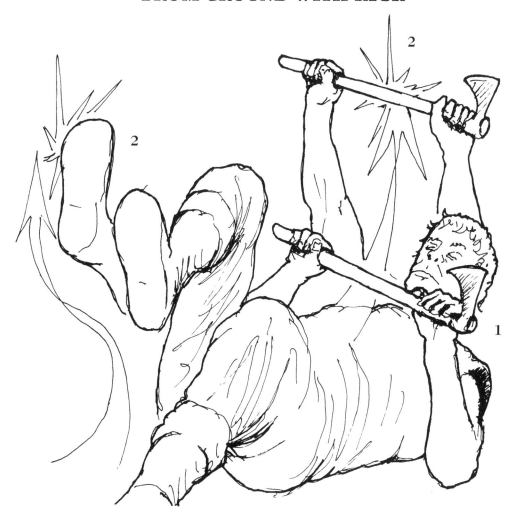

The drawing below depicts another frontal block delivered from your back at a blow directed at the groin. Note that it is necessary to rise almost to the sitting position to achieve full protection. Again, the block is followed with a kick.

Incoming blow

**FRONTAL BLOCK AGAINST BLOW TO GROIN WITH KICK**

To employ the horizontal block from the ground, raise the knee on the side of the attack and twist the torso forcefully in that direction. Simultaneously swing the opposite leg across and deliver a kick. Do this in reverse for an attack in the opposite direction.

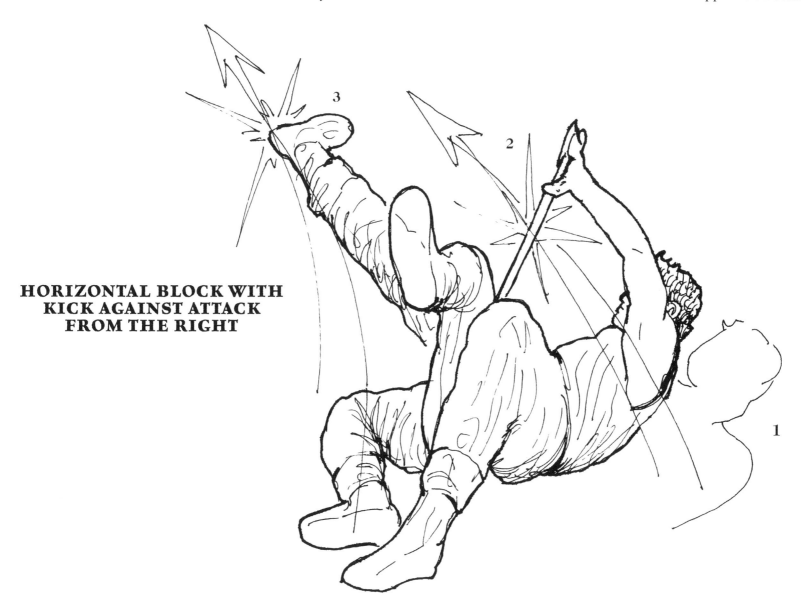

**HORIZONTAL BLOCK WITH KICK AGAINST ATTACK FROM THE RIGHT**

## HORIZONTAL BLOCK WITH KICK AGAINST ATTACK FROM LEFT

# TRAINING NOTE ON THE FRONTAL AND HORIZONTAL BLOCK DRILL

Visualize these blocks as being executed against attacks coming from the eight angles of attack discussed in the previous drills. The diagram below shows this drill.

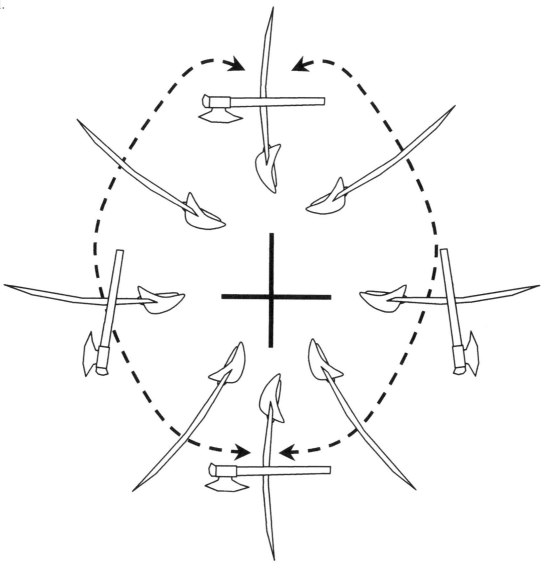

# EXECUTING THE FRONTAL HORIZONTAL DRILL

**Training Task:** Execute the frontal and horizontal block drill upright and on the ground.

**Training Condition:** You are given an anatomical silhouette wall chart or mirror, a wooden or aluminum training tomahawk, and enough horizontal and vertical space to perform the sequence safely.

**Training Standard:** Execute the drill (standing upright and on the ground) a minimum of five repetitions 3 days a week.

1. Position yourself in a frontal stance with the tomahawk held across the chest at the ready.
2. Visualize an overhead blow coming in. Drive the arms forcefully upward to block, while simultaneously sliding forward to support the block. Visualize your opponent immediately pulling back his blow and executing an upward strike to your groin. Swing the leg closest to the blow immediately to the rear while driving the tomahawk handle down to block the upcoming strike. Immediately visualize a horizontal blow incoming from the left to your midsection. Execute a horizontal block and note that your opponent pulls back and immediately executes a horizontal strike from the right. Twist in that direction and execute a horizontal block.
3. Drop to the ground on your back. Visualize your opponent's stepping over you and executing a strike to your head. Execute a frontal block followed by a kick. Your opponent steps back and executes a strike to your groin. Lean forward and execute a frontal block, followed by a kick. As your opponent attempts to kick you on the right side, twist in that direction and execute a horizontal block. Repeat this block to the left, visualizing a strike from that direction.
4. The drill should be performed sequentially from upright to the ground as one continuous action.
5. Working with a partner. No training program is fully complete without practice against a variety of different weapons. This is of particular benefit when incorporated into partner drills. Up to this point I have shown the tomahawk in use against the saber, cuttoe, and war club. Now, the training partner is equipped with a wooden rifle and simulated bayonet.

   a. Executing the drill with a partner
      i. Begin with each partner positioned opposite each other at a medium range that favors the use of the bayonet.
      ii. The exercise begins with the rifle partner executing an overhead slash at his partner head. The tomahawk partner executes a frontal block.
      iii. The rifle partner pulls back, disengaging his rifle, and sweeps a vertical butt stroke to the groin. Immediately the tomahawk partner shifts one of his legs to the rear and executes a downward frontal block.
      iv. The rifleman disengages and executes a horizontal bayonet slash to the tomahawk partner's right side. The tomahawk man executes a horizontal block in that direction.
      v. The rifleman executes an immediate horizontal butt stroke to the tomahawk man's left side. The latter twists to deliver a horizontal block in that direction.
      vi. The exercise may be continued with the rifleman closing, executing a trip. The tomahawk man drops to his back and repeats the drill from the ground position.

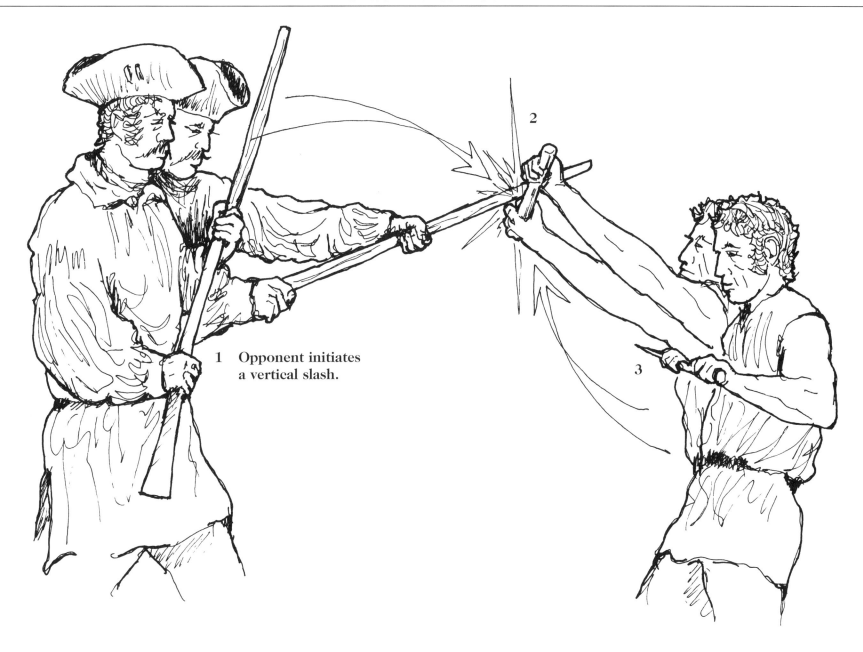

1  Opponent initiates a vertical slash.

2

3

4

6

# The Long Knife

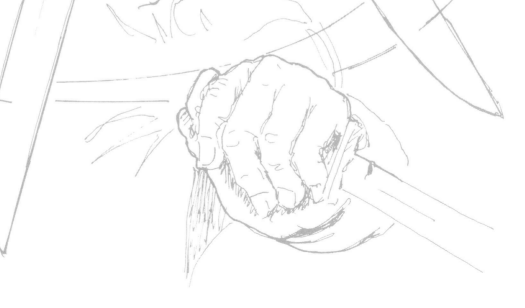

## BOOK 2

**T**he long knife was often used as a companion weapon to the tomahawk. In this section, I discuss the basics that are essential to using the long knife singly or in conjunction with the tomahawk. The basics of big-knife fighting using the saber grip were covered in my previous book, *Bowie and Big Knife Fighting System*. To complement that text, here I address the use of the long knife with the reverse grip as it would be used in the left hand. **NOTE:** Some saber-grip techniques will be shown in the engagement sequences in Book Three.

# Chapter 15

# BRIEF HISTORY OF THE LONG KNIFE

Throughout the first 200 years of this nation's history, virtually no commercial production of knives existed, for a variety of political and economic reasons. Thus, almost all commercially made knives were imported. These imports were relatively expensive and, in some cases, too fragile for demanding frontier use. To meet the need for more long knives, local blacksmiths, gunsmiths, wheelwrights, and edged-tool makers took up the additional trade of making knives.

Their knives were of simple, straightforward designs that, while very crude in appearance, were totally utilitarian. The diversity of blades created by these local craftsmen was so great that it is difficult to categorize them by a specific set of names. For our use here, I call them small, medium, and long knives.

The blade length of small knives was from 2 to 3 inches. Small knives were often referred to "patch knives" because of their use in cutting patches for the muzzleloading weapons of the time. Medium knives had 4- to 7-inch blades and were commonly thought of as "hunting knives." Some were carried in sheaths attached to the back of hunting pouches or in "possibles bags" and referred to as "bag knives." Blades for long knives were 7 to 12 inches in length, and these knives were sometimes referred to as "rifleman's knives."

## THE LOOK OF THE LONG KNIFE

The long knife of the early riflemen was made heavier than most imported knives and daggers. Most came to a relatively sharp point that sometimes had the clip point of the large Bowie knives of the 19th century. Most had a very substantial crossguard with a bone or wooden handle. The long knife was a truly multifunctional blade, serving as both a tool and a weapon. At left is one long-knife design.

# Chapter 16

# GRIPS

There are two basic grips that can be used with the long knife: the saber and reverse.

## SABER GRIP

As mentioned earlier, *Bowie and Big Knife Fighting System* provides fundamental instruction on the use of one type of long knife, the Bowie. Some historians feel that the designs of the 1840 Bowie evolved from the rifleman's knives of the early colonial period. At any rate for this book, I limit my discussion on the saber grip to its use with the engagement sequences associated with the tomahawk.

Today people are still asking which is the superior knife fighting grip, the saber or the reverse? This debate goes back and forth with much zeal because both sides probably are just too lazy to learn the advantages and disadvantages of each grip. The basic element to remember here is that a true knife expert will train to use both grips to capitalize on the advantages in specific situations. The saber grip works best with a medium to large knife. With the long knife it puts a foot of steel in front to ward off the attack and reduce range to the target. The disadvantage of the saber grip is that it is sometimes awkward to

draw the weapon with the left hand when the tomahawk is in the right; consequently, you are somewhat limited to using the back. Section 1 of *Bowie and Big Knife Fighting System* provides further information on the saber grip.

**SABER GRIP IN LEFT AND RIGHT HAND**

## REVERSE GRIP

Today modern methods lean toward the theory that the use of the knife in a reverse grip is best suited to small and medium blades. Although this theory is basically true from the practical viewpoint, no historical evidence from the Renaissance exists that this grip was also used with long knives and daggers. Some of these texts listed below may have influenced the application of the reverse grip in the American colonies:

- Fiore dei Liberi, *Flos Duellatorum*, 1410
- Hans Talhoffer, *Alte Armatur und Ringkunst*, 1459
- *Goliath* (author unknown), 1500
- Achille Marozzo, *Opera Nova*, 1536
- Paulus Hector Mair, *Opus amplissimum de arte athletica*, 1550
- Nicholas Petter, *Worstel-Konst*, 1674

These texts defined and demonstrated the advantages of this grip as (1) speed of draw and ready access to the knife handle, (2) application of pommel strikes and follow-up stabs, (3) capability for limited trapping and passing, and (4) potential to use the blade in locking and immobilizing techniques. On the next few pages I will expand on these and define the limitations as the grip is applied to the use of the long knife with the tomahawk.

The illustration on page 117 gives two methods of presenting the blade in reverse grip: edge forward and heel forward. The edge-forward presentation (left) is best suited to an offensive style of fighting. The edge faces the opponent and is particularly effective for delivering palm-up or palm-down vertical and horizontal slashes, as well as stabs. The heel-forward presentation (right) is more suited to a defensive or counter mode of fighting. Although it is well suited to the stab, its slashing capability is limited to the picking cut and the pull cut.

The drawing of the edge-forward presentation also shows the capping technique, where the thumb is placed over the end of the pommel. This is normally used to prevent the hand from sliding forward on knives with no guard when impact is made during a stab. Capping may also be used to apply additional force to a stab.

## REVERSE GRIP IN LEFT AND RIGHT HAND

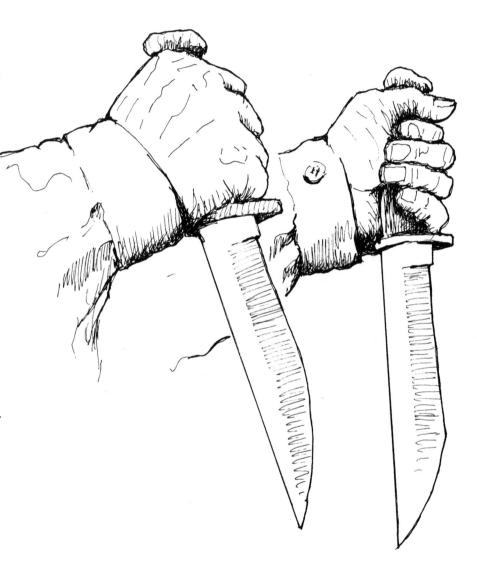

## EDGE-FORWARD AND HEEL-FORWARD PRESENTATIONS

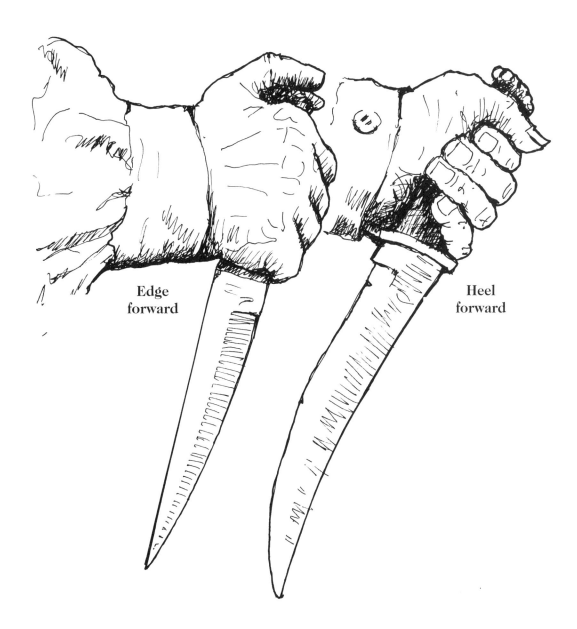

Edge
forward

Heel
forward

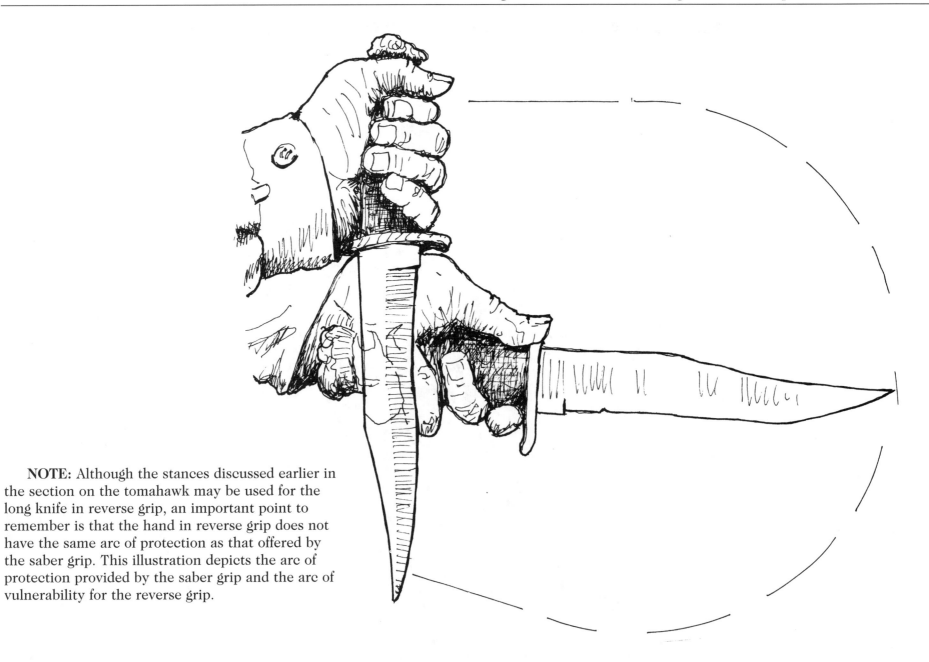

**NOTE:** Although the stances discussed earlier in the section on the tomahawk may be used for the long knife in reverse grip, an important point to remember is that the hand in reverse grip does not have the same arc of protection as that offered by the saber grip. This illustration depicts the arc of protection provided by the saber grip and the arc of vulnerability for the reverse grip.

## SLASHING (OR CUTTING) TECHNIQUES FOR REVERSE GRIP IN LEFT HAND

The slash for the reverse grip is a circular motion that begins with the fist driving forward from a chamber or half-chamber position. The wrist turns inward, presenting the edge of the blade, which is then pulled through the target. There are basically four types of slashes: (1) palm down, (2) palm up, (3) palm right, and (4) palm left. These slashes may be delivered from several angles at various high-, mid-, and lowline target areas, as illustrated.

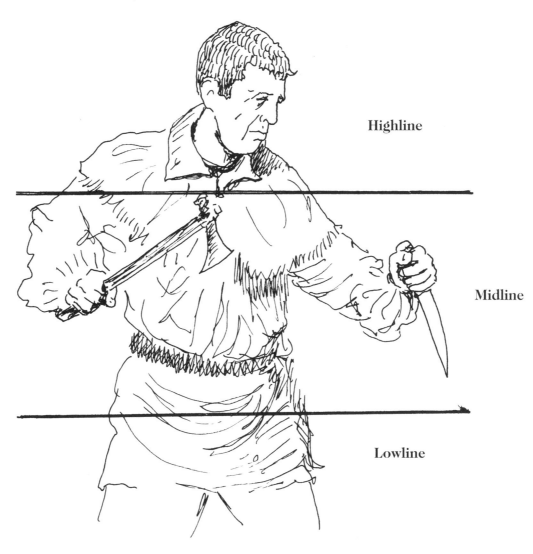

Highline

Midline

Lowline

## PALM-DOWN SLASH AGAINST HIGHLINE TARGET

## PALM-DOWN SLASH AGAINST MIDLINE TARGET

## PALM-UP SLASH AGAINST HIGHLINE TARGET

## PALM-UP SLASH AGAINST LOWLINE TARGET

## PALM-RIGHT SLASH AGAINST LOWLINE TARGET

## PALM-LEFT SLASH AGAINST HIGHLINE TARGET

# Chapter 17

# FLOURISHING

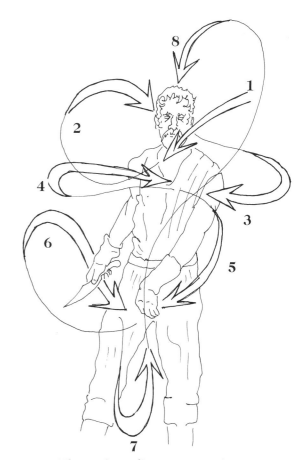

*He raised his thirsty weapon higher and held it with a firmer grasp. His eyes flashed fire. His entire attitude became more threatening; but I advanced faster and faster until I rushed full upon him, when he began to slash and saber me with his long knife at a murderous rate; first, wiping me over my shoulders, and then under my arms and across my ribs. . . .*

—A 1700s account by a frontier hunter named Bishop of his fight with an assailant named Shearman, who was equipped with a long knife (excerpted from Mark Baker's *The Sons of the Trackless Forest*)

The technique Shearman used against Bishop clearly follows a military technique called *flourishing*. This technique, normally associated with the backsword or saber, is based on a series of angles from which cutting attacks may be delivered. The flourish is accomplished by delivering one angle of attack after another in a flowing pattern. These angles are seen in numerous variations in period sword manuals from the 1400s through the 1800s, and this encounter is probably one of the more convincing pieces of evidence associating European sword techniques with the use of big fighting knives. The following drawing demonstrates the flow pattern of the flourish used by Shearman against Bishop. Section Three of *Bowie and Big Knife Fighting System* provides detailed training guidance on the use of the angles of attack (flourish) with the saber grip. In this text I demonstrate this concept using the reverse grip.

**Flourish or flow pattern for the eight angles of attack with a slash**

127

## THE EIGHT-ANGLE FLOURISHING DRILL

As mentioned earlier, the eight angles of attack have been around since the late medieval period, as evidenced in the works of Fiore dei Liberi, Achille Marozzo, and others. When it comes to practicing authentic historical knife techniques, the use of the 7, 8, 12, or 15 angles is just about as close as we can get. History also shows these angles linked together into a drill sequence that can be repeated regularly in training sessions to enhance retention of the skills. In 1821 Matheson used this flourishing technique to teach the broad- and backswords of the period.

The drill is normally performed in four figure-eight patterns. One pattern descends diagonally across the opponent's neck from right to left. The second pattern crosses the arms horizontally from right to left, and the third descends diagonally across the opponent's upper or lower leg. The fourth figure-eight pattern ascends vertically through the opponent's groin and then descends across his face. Each of the first three figure eights is executed first with a palm-down cut and immediately followed with a palm-up cut. The fourth figure-eight begins with a palm-right vertical cut followed by a palm-left downward cut. Again, in this text we are working with the left hand. The following pages contain a detailed diagram of the eight-angle flourishing drill adapted to the reverse-grip technique and a set of training tasks that may be used to develop left-handed proficiency to complement the tomahawk.

### Executing the Eight-Angle Flourishing Drill

**Training Task:** Position yourself in a frontal or weak-side-forward stance with the long knife in the left hand and the tomahawk in the right and execute the eight-angle flourishing drill with reverse grip.

**Training Condition:** You are given an anatomical silhouette wall chart or mirror, a wooden or aluminum training knife, and enough horizontal and vertical space to perform the sequence safely.

**Training Standard:** Execute the drill a minimum of five repetitions 3 days a week. For variety, execute one of the repetitions from a kneeling position.

• • •

**Action 1:** Visualize that you have just executed a base deflection of an incoming angle 2 attack with your tomahawk. Execute a palm-down descending slash across the opponent's throat (angle 1). Immediately rotate the wrist to a palm-up position and execute a descending slash across the opponent's throat (angle 2).

**Action 2:** Visualize that you have just executed a base deflection of an incoming angle 3 attack with the tomahawk. Execute a palm-down horizontal slash across the opponent's arms or midsection. Immediately rotate the wrist to a palm-up position and execute a horizontal slash across the opponent's arms or midsection.

**Action 3:** Visualize that you have just executed an edge deflection against a lowline angle 5 attack with the tomahawk. Execute a palm-down slash to the opponent's abdomen or arm. Immediately rotate the wrist to palm-up position and execute a slash back to the left.

**Action 4:** Visualize that you have executed a base deflection against an overhead angle 8 attack. Execute a vertical palm-right upward slash to the opponent's groin. Immediately rotate the pommel to the right and do a vertical downward slash to the face. Illustrations of these actions are on the following eight pages.

# EIGHT-ANGLE FLOURISHING DRILL WITH REVERSE GRIP (LEFT HAND)
## Highline Figure-Eight Pattern Angle 1 (Palm Down)

## Highline Figure-Eight Pattern Angle 2 (Palm Up)

## Midline Figure-Eight Pattern Angle 3 (Palm Down)

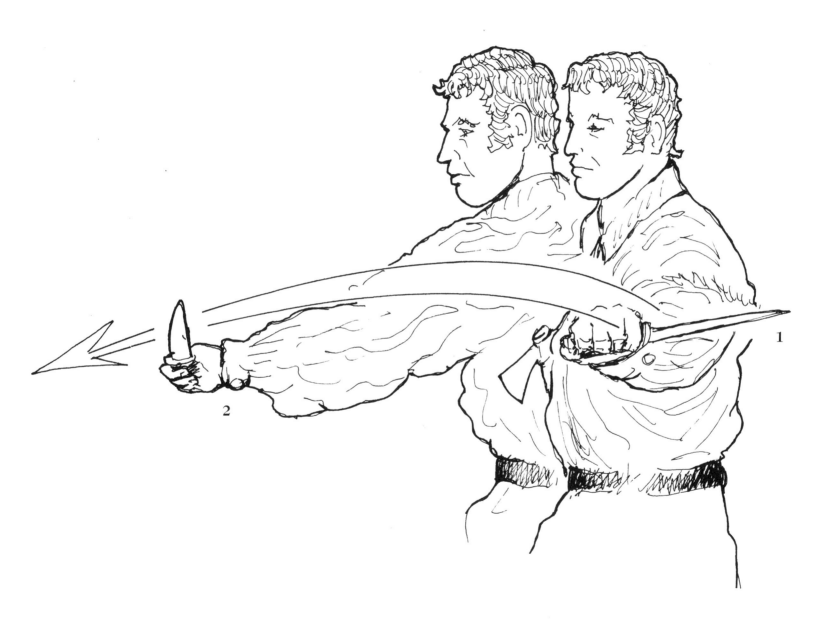

## Midline Figure-Eight Pattern Angle 4 (Palm Up)

## Lowline Figure-Eight Pattern Angle 5 (Palm Down)

## Lowline Figure-Eight Pattern Angle 6 (Palm Up)

## Vertical Upward Cut of the Figure-Eight Pattern Angle 7 (Palm Right)

## Vertical Downward Cut of the Figure-Eight Pattern Angle 8 (Palm Left)

## USING A WALL CHART FOR THE EIGHT-ANGLE FLOURISHING DRILL

Most of the medieval and Renaissance masters depicted the basic cutting angles as a diagram with angles or as a simple wall chart with the angles superimposed on a human silhouette. Often in their manuals, we see drawings of a student practicing his cuts before such a chart with a watchful instructor standing by. The wall chart shown on page 138 is designed for such use. It is recommended that this chart be enlarged to life size using a series of grids or a reproduction device.

**Visual from Jakob Sutter's 1612 text depicting the eight-angle wall chart as an instructional aid**

# WALL CHART FOR THE EIGHT-ANGLE FLOURISHING DRILL

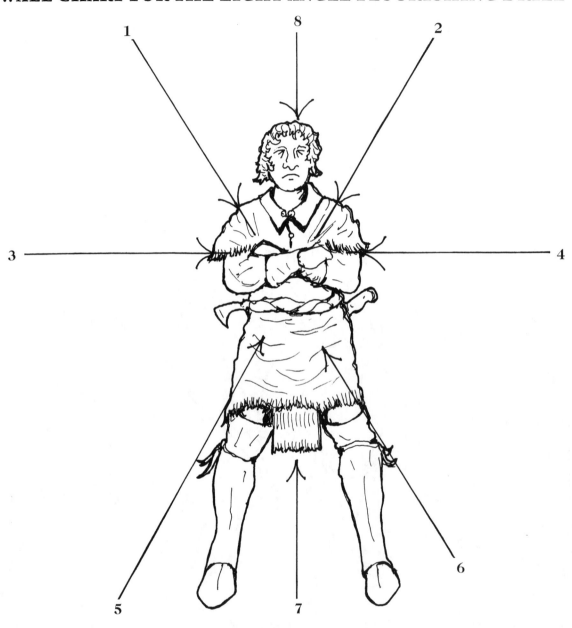

## WORKING THE FLOURISHING DRILL ON A WALL CHART

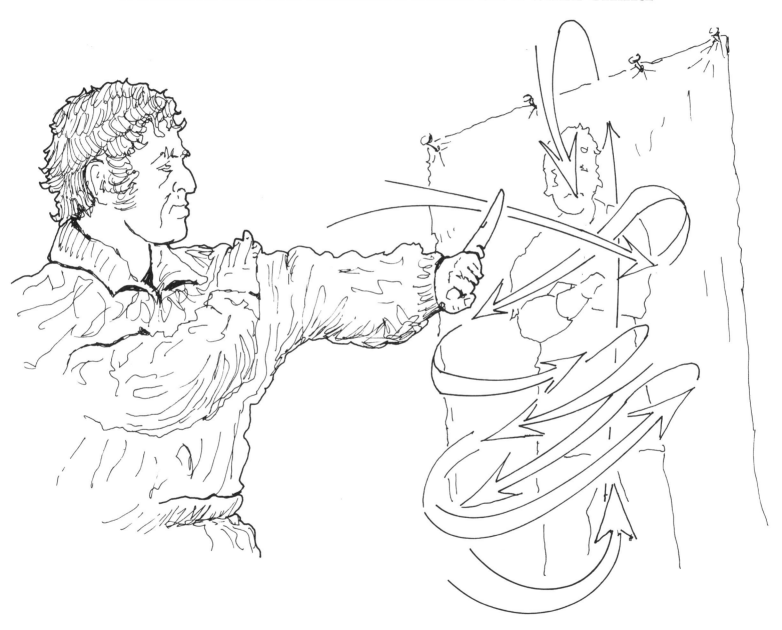

## SLASH WORK ON A PELL

To truly understand the delivery and follow-through aspect of a slash, there is really nothing better than to practice the eight-angle flourishing drill against a pell. This is particularly important for obtaining proficiency in delivering the palm-up horizontal slash. The ergonomic aspect of this technique is awkward and requires shifting the body away from the slash to obtain an accurate horizontal angle and forceful cutting action.

Pell work should be done a minimum of 3 days a week. Focus should be placed on delivering full-force, accurate angle 6 and 7 slashes from the kneeling position and then quickly rising to the upright position to deliver angle 8. This sequence is depicted on the following pages.

## ANGLE 6 PALM-UP SLASH FROM KNEELING POSITION

## ANGLE 7 PALM-RIGHT SLASH FROM A KNEELING POSITION

## ANGLE 8 PALM-LEFT SLASH FROM A STANDING POSITION

## PULL-CUT

The pull-cut is another type of slashing/cutting technique that is preformed with the heel-forward reverse grip. This cut, while limited in its application, is particularly effective in attacking the limbs of the opponent at close quarters. The pull-cut is normally executed in three actions: (1) the blade is driven forward, past, or over the target; (2) the hand is dropped momentarily onto the target with blade now behind; and (3) the blade, now with its edge on the target, is pulled violently back in the direction it came, nastily slicing through muscles or ligaments. The illustration below depicts a pull-cut to an opponent's leg.

1

Hook behind opponent's hand

Pull

2

Edge

3

Back

Through

## CLOSE-UP OF THE PULL-CUT TECHNIQUE AGAINST AN OPPONENT'S HAND

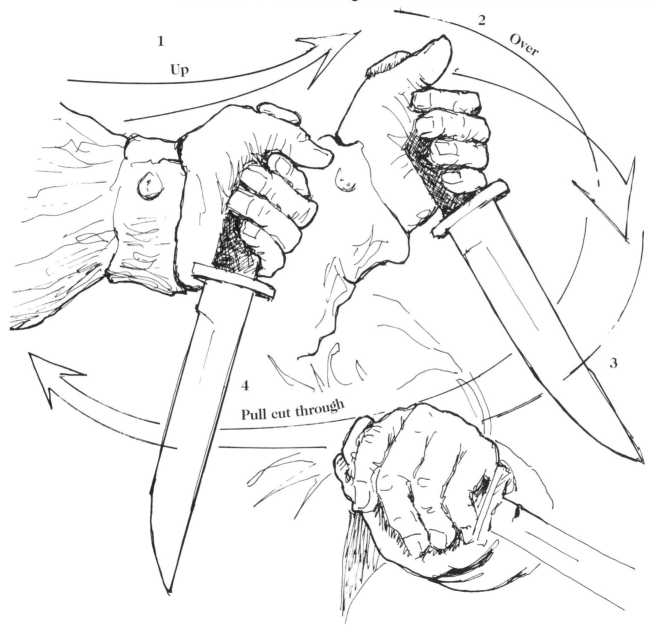

## PICK-CUT

The pick-cut may be performed with either the edge or heel forward in the reverse grip. The execution of this cut involves driving the hand rapidly forward or over the target a short distance and then immediately snapping the wrist forward, which pulls the first inch of the point or blade back through the target. Because the pick-cut is not a high-impact strike, it does not produce massive wounds. Rather, it is best used to distract an opponent with strikes to the hands or blinding cuts to the eye.

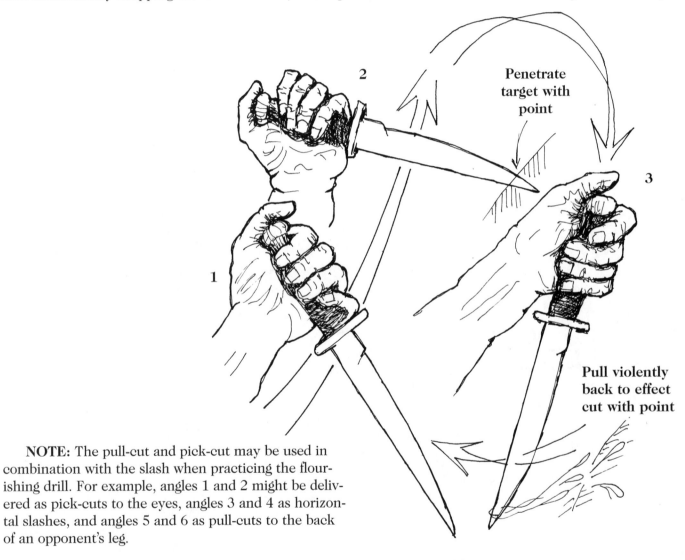

Penetrate target with point

Pull violently back to effect cut with point

**NOTE:** The pull-cut and pick-cut may be used in combination with the slash when practicing the flourishing drill. For example, angles 1 and 2 might be delivered as pick-cuts to the eyes, angles 3 and 4 as horizontal slashes, and angles 5 and 6 as pull-cuts to the back of an opponent's leg.

# Chapter 18

# THE STAB

In terms of power and the ability to deliver deep, penetrating wounds, the reverse-grip stab is probably the most effective technique. To execute a stab, keep the forearm and wrist in line while bending the elbow. Swing the arm forward with a hammerlike motion, driving the point into the target. These may be performed as overhand descending, horizontal, and underhand ascending stabs. As with the slash, the reverse-grip stab may be performed through eight angles into various target areas. The reverse-grip stab was used extensively in medieval dagger techniques, which may have come to the American colonies by word of mouth. The drawings at right are adapted from Fiore dei Liberi's *Flos Duellatorum* and depict early reverse-grip stabbing and counter-stabbing work.

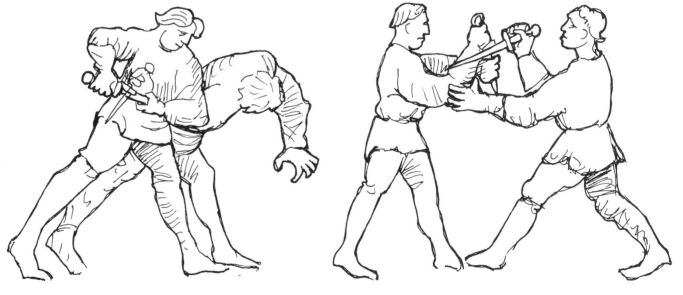

## OVERHAND STAB

The overhand stab was frequently shown in 18th- and 19th-century drawings of Indian attacks on the colonists. Usually these depict a helpless settler fleeing from an Indian whose arm is raised to deliver the overhand stab. This technique is also frequently referred to in contemporary written accounts. Targets for the over-hand stab are usually the head, eyes, and neck. This stab is frequently delivered following a trap by the opposite hand, where the opponent's guarding arm is pushed down or against his body. The drawing below depicts this technique.

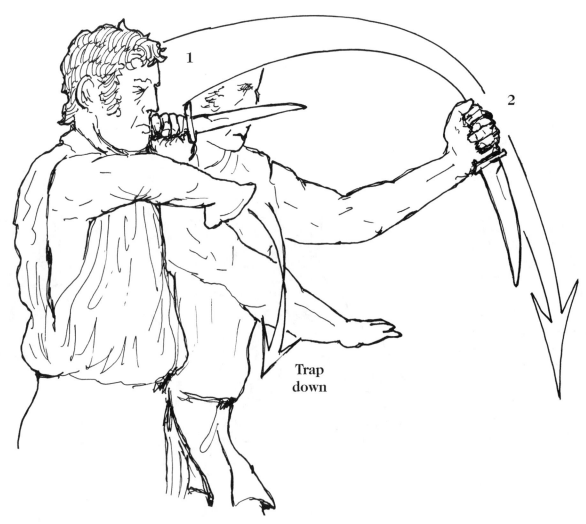

Trap down

## CLOSE-UP VIEW OF OVERHAND STAB

## HORIZONTAL STAB

The horizontal stab is executed by placing the blade hand across the chest over the right breast. The arm is extended forcefully outward with the palm down and blade generally horizontal to the ground. This stab may also be performed from left to right with the palm up. However, as is shown later, this requires the body and legs to be shifted to the left to allow the point to come to bear on the target. Targets for this technique are usually the rib and kidney areas. The drawing below shows the horizontal stab performed from the right (across the chest) to the left.

## CLOSE-UP VIEW OF HORIZONTAL STAB

## UNDERHAND STAB

The underhand stab is as powerful as it is deceptive. Because it is usually initiated from a low line outside the opponent's field of vision, it is often not seen until it is too late. The stab is initiated by dropping the blade hand below the belt line and then striking force-fully upward and out. This stab is often used when withdrawing from an onrushing opponent intent on striking the head. The technique is demonstrated below.

## CLOSE-UP VIEW OF UNDERHAND STAB

# TRAINING OBJECTIVE: THE EIGHT ANGLES OF STAB WITH A REVERSE GRIP

As with the cut, the stab may be practiced against areas that correspond to the eight angles of attack. The angles of attack for the reverse-grip stab are the following:

**Angle 1:** An overhand stab to the opponent's right shoulder or neck area

**Angle 2:** An overhand stab to the opponent's left shoulder or neck area

**Angle 3:** A palm-up horizontal stab to the opponent's right arm, ribs, or chest

**Angle 4:** A palm-down horizontal stab to the opponent's left arm, ribs, or chest

**Angle 5:** A palm-up horizontal stab to the opponent's right leg or groin

**Angle 6:** A palm-down horizontal stab to the opponent's left leg or groin

**Angle 7:** An underhand vertical stab to the opponent's groin

**Angle 8:** An overhand vertical stab to the opponent's face or head

Training with these angles should be performed first as figure-eight patterns that consist of executing angles 1 and 2, 3 and 4, 5 and 6, and then 7 and 8, as individual two-strike patterns. Once you have mastered this, the attack flow should be expanded to encompass all eight angle stabs. The wall chart illustrated earlier may be used to practice these stabs. Shown at right are the angles of attack for the left hand.

**ANGLES OF ATTACK FOR LEFT HAND**

# EIGHT-ANGLE STAB WITH A LEFT-HAND REVERSE GRIP

## Angles 1 and 2 Pattern

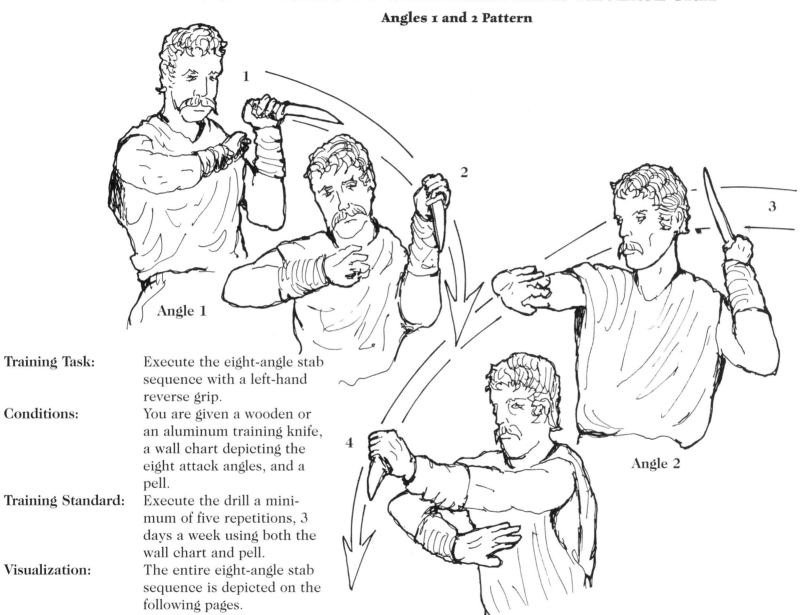

Angle 1

Angle 2

**Training Task:** Execute the eight-angle stab sequence with a left-hand reverse grip.

**Conditions:** You are given a wooden or an aluminum training knife, a wall chart depicting the eight attack angles, and a pell.

**Training Standard:** Execute the drill a minimum of five repetitions, 3 days a week using both the wall chart and pell.

**Visualization:** The entire eight-angle stab sequence is depicted on the following pages.

## Angles 3 and 4 Pattern

Angle 3

Angle 4

## Angles 5 and 6 Pattern

Angle 5

Angle 6

## Angles 7 and 8 Pattern

Angle 7

1

2

3

4

Angle 8

**TRAINING NOTE:** It has been said that reverse-grip techniques for the long knife are characterized by multiple attacks against more than one target area. This often consists of first delivering a slash, followed immediately with a stab, or vice versa. Because training for these engagements may be done using the same eight-angle drills addressed previously, our discussion here will be limited to the examples below and in the combat scenarios that combine the long knife with the tomahawk. The full aspects of knife fighting in reverse grip are for another text. Here are some illustrations of the slash-stab combinations.

157

## DEFENSIVE OR COUNTER TECHNIQUES FOR REVERSE GRIP IN LEFT HAND

Any review of medieval or Renaissance dagger techniques that may have been brought to America reveals some fairly consistent methods for reverse-grip knife fighting. Dei Liberi's *Flos Duellatorum*, *Codex Wallerstein* (1470), *Goliath*, and Mair's *Opus amplissimum de arte athletica* are a few of the period manuscripts that demonstrate this standardization in the areas of dagger and counter-dagger techniques. Three basic skills that are as applicable today as at they were at the time they were described are the block, scissors catch, and bridge. Please note that for simplicity's sake I use the more descriptive common names for these techniques rather than period terminology. These techniques are used in combination with a variety of pushing, pinning, catching, and levering actions against armed and unarmed opponents.

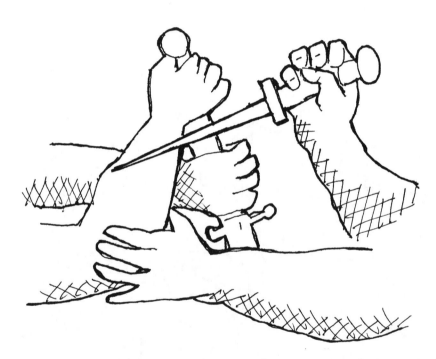

From Fiore dei Liberi's *Flos Duellatorum* demonstrating the press and bridge technique

### The Block

The reverse-grip block is executed by quickly pushing the hand forward in a motion similar to punching with an empty fist. The hand is directed slightly left, right, or above the target so that the blade will encounter the opponent's hand, wrist, forearm, or upper arm. Blocking with the reverse grip is as unique as it is dangerous. It requires a lot more training and practice than that associated with the saber grip.

Remember the earlier discussion of the arc of vulnerability when comparing reverse-grip with saber-grip knife fighting? This is particularly so when executing any block. The key aspect to remember for all reverse-grip blocking is the exposure of the hand. Care must be taken to ensure that an opponent does not redirect his attack to hit the exposed hand. Blocks can also be executed to hit against the opponent's incoming weapon, but you must also ensure that the force of the blow does not slide off your own blade and go into the arm. This can usually be avoided by shifting the body away from the incoming blow when executing the block.

Along the same lines, you should never think of a block as a static, halting action. Rather, all blocks should be followed immediately by a pushing action to direct the opponent's weapon arm away from his intended target. This press or push action is essential when following a block with a counterattack from a weapon in the opposite hand. The next illustration shows some of the fundamental aspects of the reverse-grip block used with the left hand.

## BLOCKING AND SHIFTING

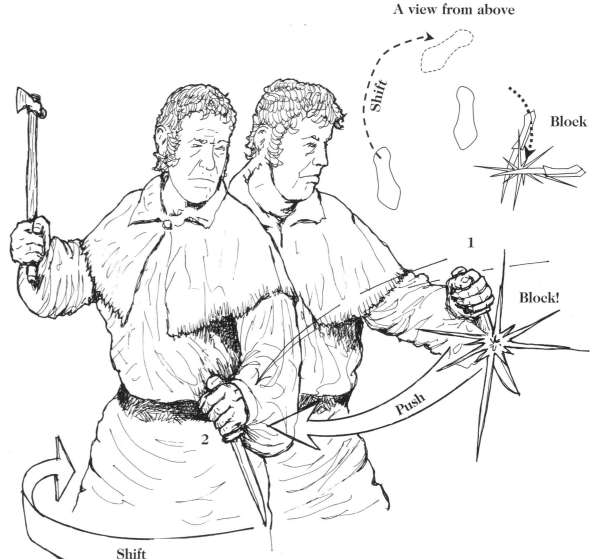

A view from above

Shift

Block

1

Block!

Push

2

Shift

**159**

***Targeting the Block***

Blocks may be aimed at the left or right side of the incoming weapon, hand, wrist, or arm. Whenever possible direct the block to the opponent's hand. This often results in immediate disarming and reduces the necessity for further blocking actions. The illustration below depicts a block to the hand area that targets the fingers.

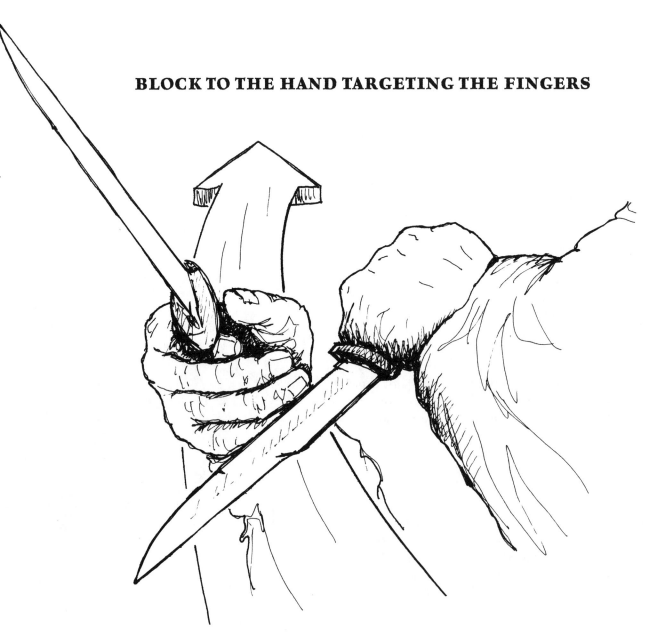

**BLOCK TO THE HAND TARGETING THE FINGERS**

# TRAINING WALL CHART FOR REVERSE-GRIP BLOCKS USING LEFT HAND

During the 1700s and 1800s, one method for retaining the basic concepts of saber cutting and parrying was the use of geometric diagrams. These gave the angles of an incoming attack and the relative positions of one's weapon to block it. Frequently, these charts were drawn from the view of the user. In keeping with this practice, I have included a modified version of a diagram that depicts the reverse-grip blocks using the left hand.

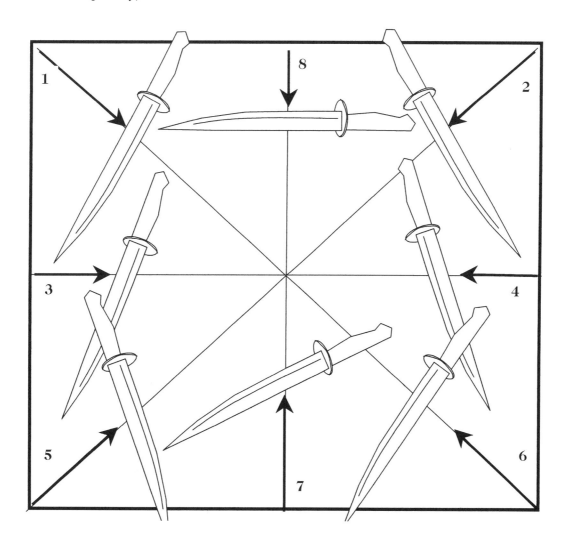

## TRAINING OBJECTIVE: EIGHT ANGLES OF BLOCKING WITH REVERSE GRIP

As with the cut and the stab, the block may be practiced against eight angles of attack. Training with these blocks should be performed against high-, mid-, and lowline attacks. The eight-angle blocking sequence consists of the following:

**Action 1:** Effect a block against the blade, hand, or forearm of an incoming angle 1 attack.
**Action 2:** Effect a block against the blade, hand, or forearm of an incoming angle 2 attack.
**Action 3:** Effect a block against the blade, hand, or forearm of an incoming angle 3 attack.
**Action 4:** Effect a block against the blade, hand, or forearm of an incoming angle 4 attack.
**Action 5:** Effect a block against the blade, hand, or forearm of an incoming angle 5 attack.
**Action 6:** Effect a block against the blade, hand, or forearm of an incoming angle 6 attack.
**Action 7:** Effect a block against the blade, hand, or forearm of an incoming angle 7 attack.
**Action 8:** Effect a block against the blade, hand, or forearm of an incoming angle 8 attack.

## BLOCKS AGAINST EIGHT-ANGLE ATTACKS FROM OPPONENT USING SABER GRIP

**Block Against Angle 1 Attack**

Foot and body shift

## Block Against Angle 2 Attack

NOTE: This may also be
performed palm down.

1

2

Foot and body shift

## Block Against Angle 3 Attack

Foot and body shift

## Block Against Angle 4 Attack

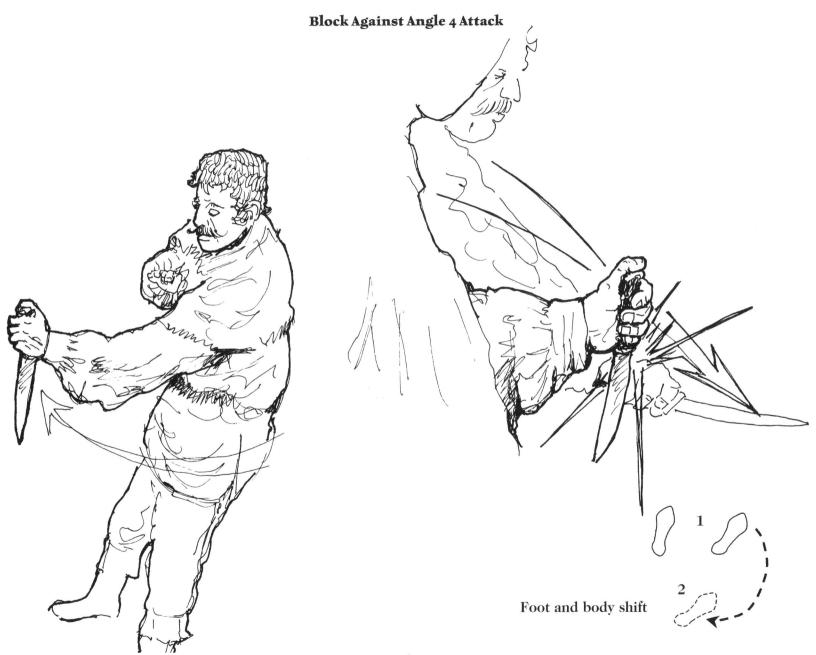

Foot and body shift

1

2

## Block Against Angle 5 Attack

Foot and body shift

## Block Against Angle 6 Attack

Foot and body shift

## Block Against Angle 7 Attack

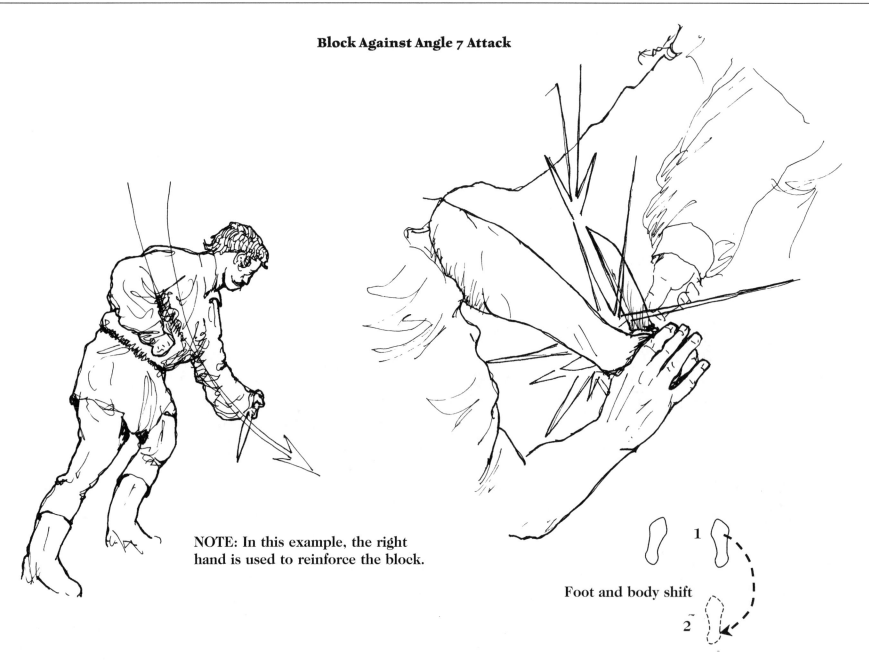

NOTE: In this example, the right hand is used to reinforce the block.

Foot and body shift

1

2

## Block Against Angle 8 Attack

NOTE: In this example the right hand is used to reinforce the block.

Foot and body shift

# Chapter 19

# THE SCISSOR CATCH

Another technique for defense with the reverse grip involves striking with the heel of the hand the wrist of an opponent delivering an incoming blow. Here the blade passes over the wrist and is pulled forcefully backward while simultaneously closing onto the wrist, as with a pair of scissors. The scissor technique may be performed with the palm up, vertical, or down, depending on which angle the attack comes from. The illustration at right shows this technique with the palm vertical.

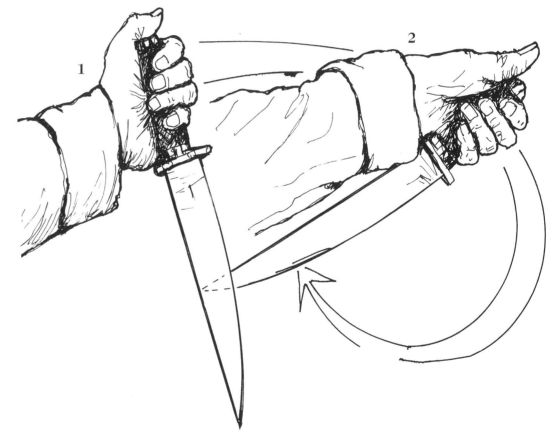

## VERTICAL SCISSOR CATCH PERFORMED ON WEAPON-BEARING ARM

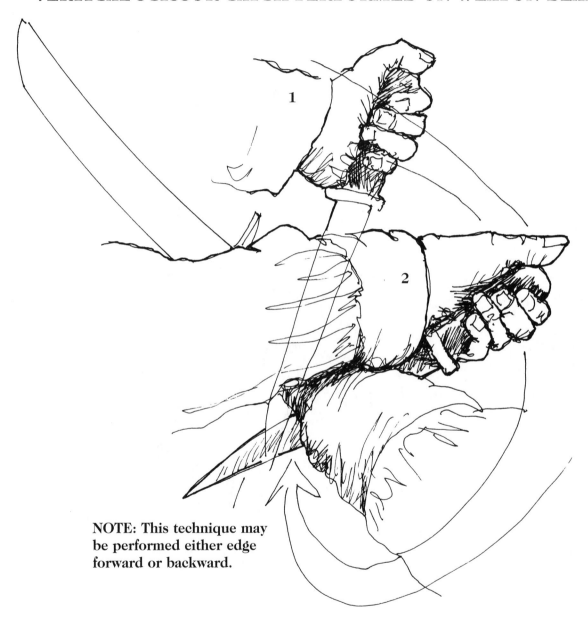

NOTE: This technique may
be performed either edge
forward or backward.

## SCISSOR CATCH PERFORMED WITH THE PALM DOWN

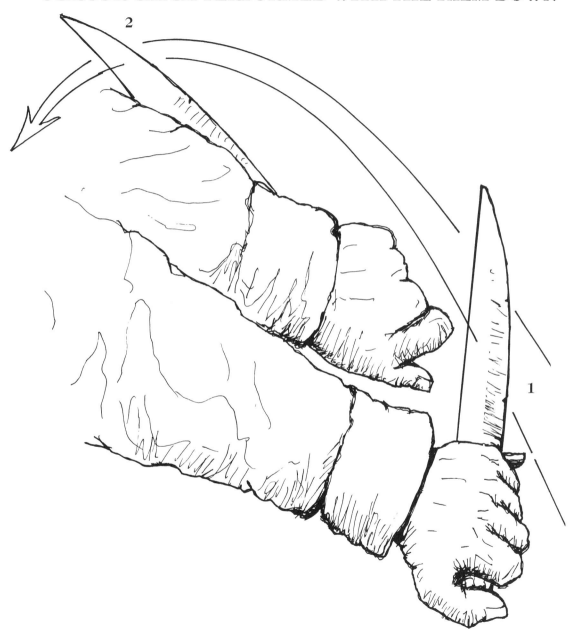

## TRAINING OBJECTIVE

As with the cut, stab, and block, the scissor catch may be practiced against eight angles of attack using the same task, conditions, and standards discussed in those chapters.

# Engagement Sets, Sequences, and Related Fighting Concepts for the Tomahawk and Long Knife

## BOOK 3

Now that the groundwork has been established for the tomahawk and long knife individually, I will outline a fighting protocol that uses these weapons independently and in unison. This protocol consists of conceptual visualizations that present the technique, sequence, and set as a visual flow, and both horizontal and overhead views.

An engagement set consists of a series of three to five techniques linked together to form a pattern. These activities may be performed as solo sets or with a partner. In some martial arts these protocols may be termed *drills*. The difference here is that an engagement set places more focus on the application of offensive and defensive techniques in relation to a given target area and fighting situation rather than the application of a repetitive preset action. Engagement sets are flexible training techniques that allow the individual to focus on the weaknesses. The training progression for any engagement set involves the following:

1.  Training solo, where the techniques are executed free in the open air with only slight foot shifting.
2.  Training on a circular floor chart, executing the techniques with full movement.
3.  Training on circular floor chart with a training partner in the center. Here the techniques are performed at half-speed with the partner feeding offensive and defensive techniques. An important point to note here is that the circular floor chart is only a training aid to assist you in grasping the concept of the technique; it is not intended to be rigidly adhered to.
4.  Training on pell with live-steel weapons. Here the pell is visualized as an opponent in the center of the circle, where techniques of attack, defense, and movement are practiced against it.

## A BRIEF PRIMER ON THE CIRCLE AS A TRAINING AID

Just as the primary training aid for the fundamentals is the wall chart, the circle provides the dynamics for engagement set training. This circle takes the form of the circular floor plan shown below. Several examples of the use of this type of training aid can be seen throughout history. The most excessive approach was in Gérard Thibault's 1628 *Academy of the Sword*. Here mathematical rules of geometry were applied to the use of straight lines, circular movements, and human proportions to describe the essential components of the Spanish system of fencing. Often referred to as a *mysterious circle*, the circumference was determined by an individual's height and applied the principles of range, timing, and angle to move the body out of danger and to create openings for either defense or offense. Because the floor plans of Thibault were complex and deeply rooted in the principles of Renaissance hermetic swordsmanship, only the concepts of creating your circle and dominating the circle are applied here to engagement set training.

### Creating Your Circle

The height of an individual determines when he is within the range of combat or the circumference of the circle. Simply put, this is the area in which you can hit your opponent or he can hit you. The illustrations on the following pages show you how to create your circle. The distance from the navel to the ground indicates the diameter of the circle, and when one rotates 360 degrees, this will form the circumference according to the individual's height. When viewed from a fighting stance, this line also can be used to visualize the range to the opponent.

### Dominating the Circle

The diameter line should be viewed as the range or centerline running from the fighting stance to

## CIRCULAR FLOOR PLAN FOR TRAINING

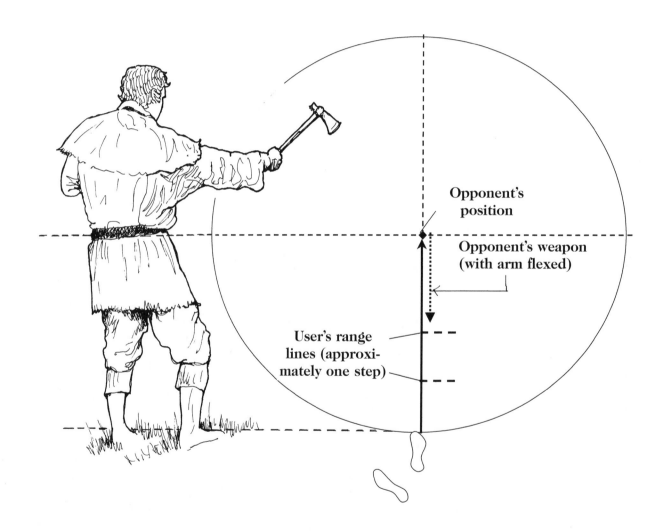

Opponent's position

Opponent's weapon (with arm flexed)

User's range lines (approximately one step)

the opponent (in the center of the circle). An important point is that shorter individuals will have a smaller circle than taller persons. Visualizing this difference when facing an opponent and taking it into account when attacking or defending may provide a decisive advantage. Along the diameter line you will note that there are two horizontal dashed lines representing approximately one step into the circle. The purpose of these reference marks are shown in the next illustration. Note that when a person steps across the "S" line into the circle he falls within the range of the opponent's weapon. The length of the weapon (X on the illustration) is a prime consideration when attempting to move or dominate an opponent's circle. To

avoid being hit or to create openings to attack, a combatant must move left or right of the diameter line.

I have only touched on the applications and aspects of circular floor plans as training aids, but I don't need to go into more detail for our purposes here. I will use this floor plan along with the drawings to depict the engagement sets and sequences for the tomahawk and long knife. The floor plans shown with each set are provided mostly as a frame of reference for the movement taking place. Remember that the floor plans, like the wall charts, are nothing more than teaching aids that should be used with great flexibility to assist in grasping the fighting concept. Do not let your strict adherence to the floor plan become an end in itself.

*"To assure yourself of the right measure (range), you must pay attention to the length of the sword and the height of your adversary—therefore keep yourself out of distance until you know how far you can reach out."*
—Lt. Thomas Mathewson, 1805

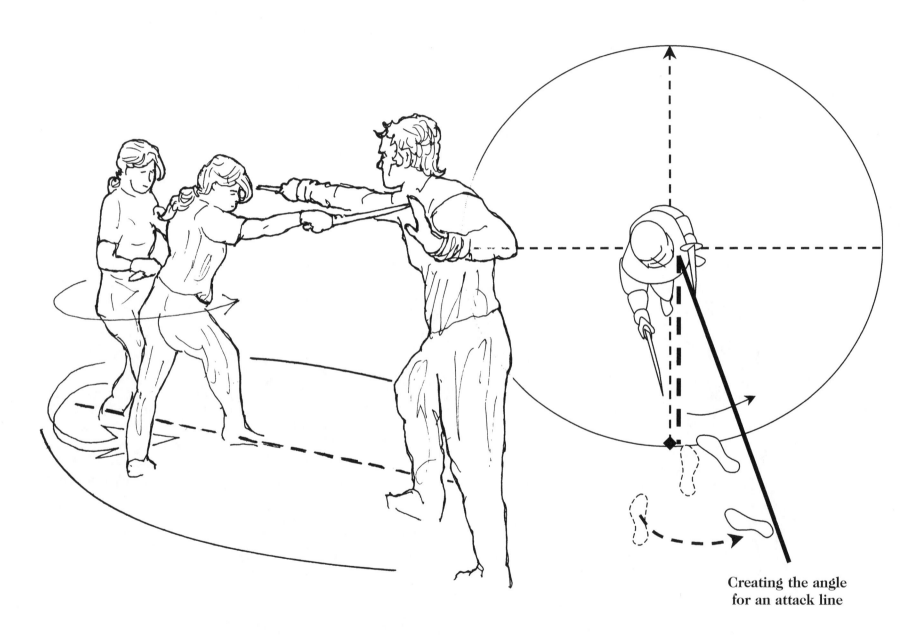

Creating the angle
for an attack line

# Chapter 20

# ENGAGEMENT SETS

## ENGAGEMENT SET 1

**Task Title:**   Chop, thrust, and chop combination

**Condition:**   Hold the tomahawk with the right hand in an extended grip, long position, and the long knife in the left hand in a saber grip.

**Execution:**

1. As a solo set
   a. Execute a chop to the opponent's neck and shoulder area.
   b. Immediately follow with a long knife straight thrust to his midsection as you move to the right away from a potential attack.
   c. Withdraw the long knife and follow with a lowline chop to his left leg or to the inside of his right leg.
   d. Standard: Repeat this drill five times each training session.
2. With a training partner

   a. The training partner should be armed with two long-knife trainers for this exercise. Care should be taken that both partners have adequate eye, throat, chest, and groin protection. This set should be executed at slow speed at least 10 times before attempting it at half speed.
   b. The set begins with your executing a chop to the opponent's head and neck. He executes a high parry with the left hand and follows with an immediate right-handed straight thrust to your midsection.
   c. As the opponent's thrust comes in, rotate your trunk, shift to the right, and deliver a straight thrust with the long knife. Continuing to move to the right, deliver a chop to his closer leg.
   d. Standard: Repeat this drill five times each training session.

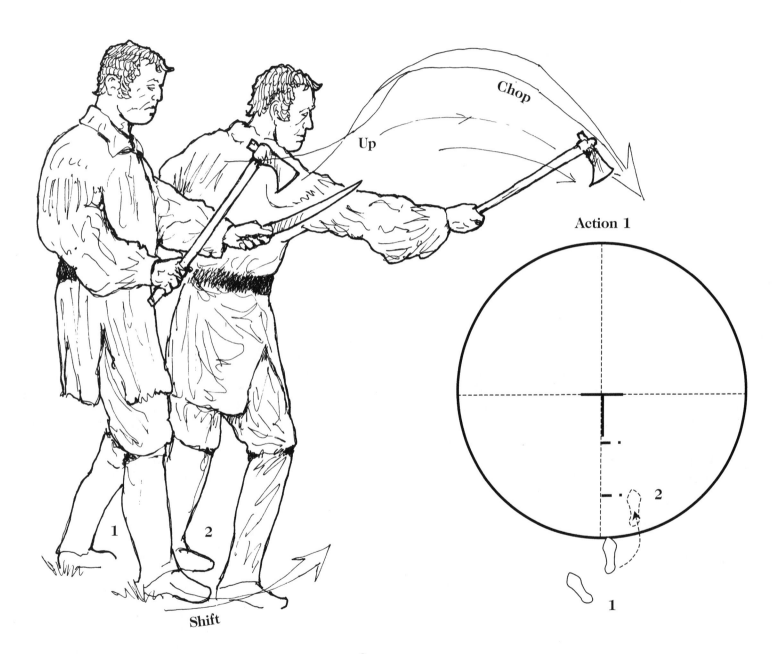

Up

Chop

Action 1

1

2

Shift

1

2

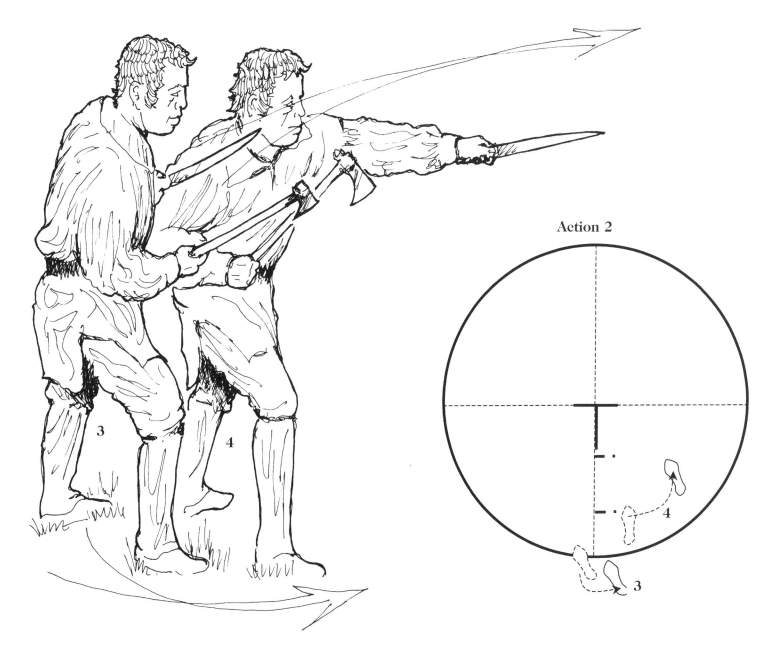

Action 2

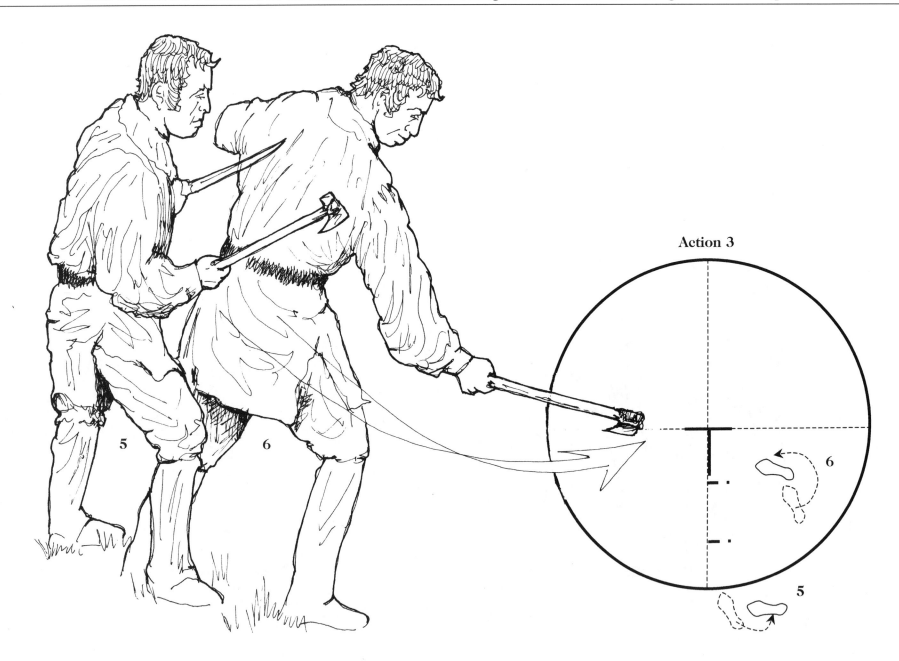

Action 3

## SEQUENCE WITH A TRAINING PARTNER

NOTE: When executing this parry, the opponent should shift slightly to his right.

*"Always keep your body straight up, except when you push. You must bend it from your adversary's point or to the contrary side from it."*
—Donald McBane, 1728

*"Calmness, vigor, and judgement."*
—Sir William Hope, 1707

Here is the shift that Donald McBane refers to on page 183. This is a very deliberate movement that takes the body out of line with the opponent's thrust. Simultaneous with the shift to the right, push the left hand with the long knife forward as a straight thrust to the opponent's shoulder, throat, or midsection. In a real fight the shift and thrust appear to happen in unison. This is a very dynamic, fast movement that can push an opponent upright.

**SAFETY NOTE:** When working this set with a partner, take care to stop the thrust short of impact or, as shown in the illustration, move the thrust slightly off target. Note that the opponent's partner also has shifted slightly to avoid impact. Again, these sets should be practiced first at slow speed and then at half speed until mastery is achieved. Under no circumstances should these be practiced at full speed without padded weapons and necessary protective equipment.

5

# ENGAGEMENT SET 2

**Task Title:** Overhead cut, hook, and trap, "around-the-head" circular chop combination. **NOTE:** The around-the-head circular chop is delivered as an angle 2 attack. The primary difference is that the tomahawk is lifted above and behind the head, following a circular path around the head before descending into angle 2. If performed properly in conjunction with the slide into the opponent, the blow may never be seen.

**Condition:** Hold the tomahawk in the right hand in an extended grip, long position, with the arm in half chamber.

**Execution:**

1. As a solo set
   a. Execute an angle 1 cut to the opponent's neck and shoulder area.
   b. With the long knife in reverse grip in the left hand, execute a downward hook over the opponent's incoming thrust arm and pull down. Simultaneously shift the torso to the left outside and away from the opponent's thrust.
   c. Slide closer to the opponent while continuing to push his arm farther down. Immediately execute an around-the-head circular chop.

2. With a training partner
   a. The training partner should be armed with two long-knife trainers. Care should be taken that both partners have adequate eye, throat, chest, and groin protection. This set should be executed at slow speed at least 10 times before attempting at half speed.
   b. The set begins with your executing an angle 1 cut. The opponent executes a high parry with the left hand and follows with an immediate thrust with the right to your throat.
   c. As the thrust comes in, rotate your trunk to the left and execute a downward hook, pulling the opponent's arm forcefully toward the ground.
   d. Sliding closer and continuing to push down on the opponent's arm, execute an around-the-head circular chop.
   e. Standard: Repeat this sequence five times each training session.

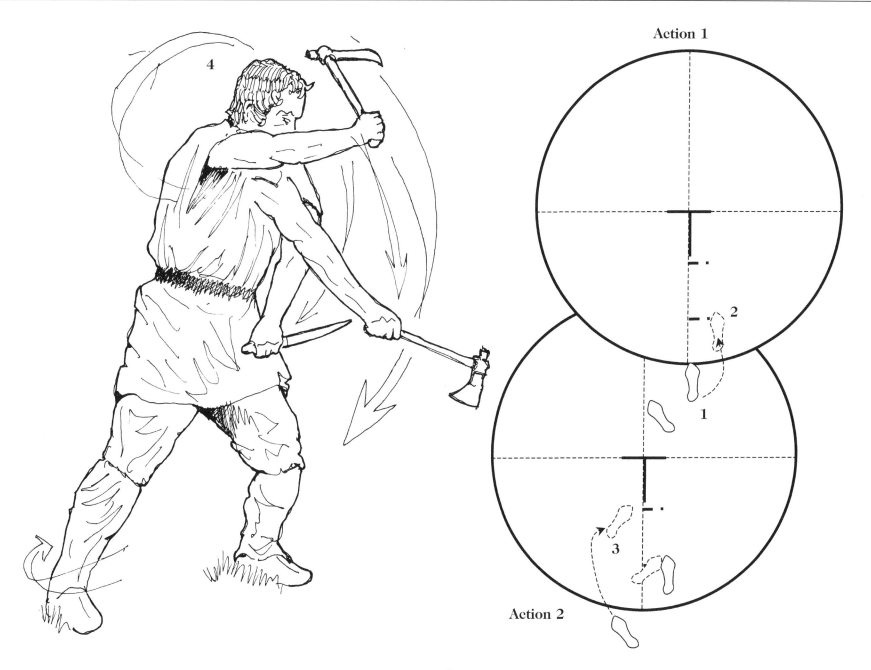

## SEQUENCE WITH A TRAINING PARTNER

*"Nothing is so difficult in fencing as to know well the measure or distance, since there are no certain rules to determine and fix it— practice and justness of the eye must give you an idea of it. It is a most essential point, and he who neglects to learn it, is most often hit in an assault."*
—Lt. Thomas Mathewson (1805)

3

# ENGAGEMENT SET 3

**Task Title:** High block/parry, crossover, horizontal slash, and over-head circular chop

**Condition:** Hold the tomahawk in the right hand in an extended grip, long position, with the arm in the extended position. Hold the long knife in the left hand in reverse grip.

**Execution:**

1. As a solo set
   a. Execute a high block/parry against an incoming angle 2 attack. Simultaneously step across with the right leg out of the angle of the opponent's strike.
   b. Step into the opponent by swinging your left leg around to the right and immediately executing a horizontal slash to the opponent's arm or throat.
   c. As this slash is completed, pull your left arm back along the same line and execute a stab.
   d. As the stab is retracted, rotate the hips to the right and execute an around-the-head circular chop to the opponent's neck or head.

2. With a training partner
   a. The training partner should be armed with a training saber. Care should be taken that both partners have adequate eye, throat, chest, and groin protection. This set should be executed at slow speed at least 10 times before attempting at half speed.
   b. The set begins with the saber-equipped training partner executing an angle 2 cut. You then execute a high block/parry while simultaneously stepping across the opponent's centerline to the left.
   c. Swing the left around, move into the opponent and deliver a slash and stab. Immediately following the stab, pin the opponent's saber arm against his body. As the opponent's arm is pinned, push it down, drive the tomahawk up, and deliver an around-the-head circular chop. **NOTE:** If required, you may deliver a midline stab after the chop.
   d. Standard: Repeat this sequence five times each training session.

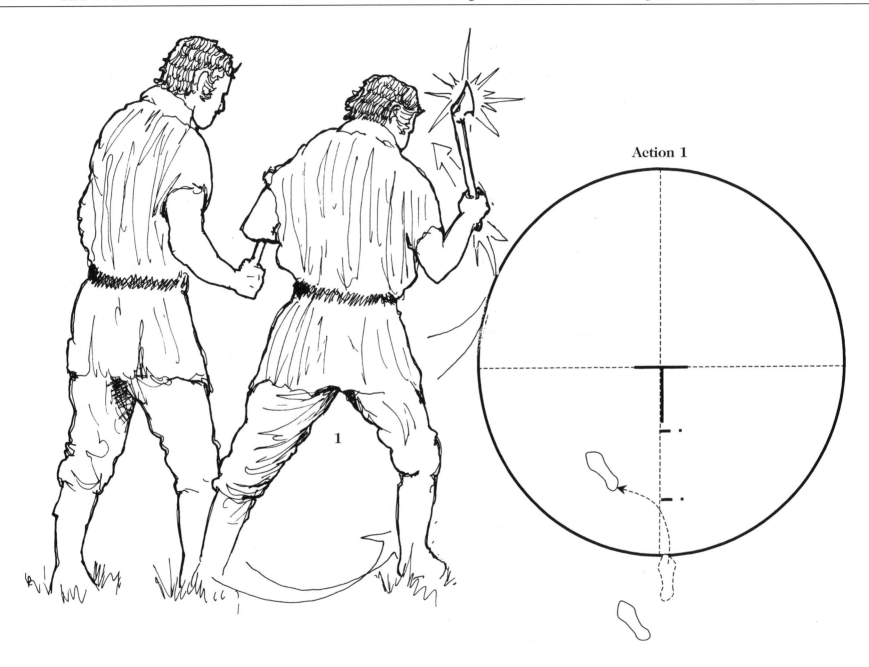

Action 1

1

Action 2

## INTEGRATION OF PELL TRAINING

Earlier I mentioned that the training progression for the engagement sets should follow this sequence: (1) open-air solo sets with no movement, (2) movement on a floor chart, and (3) training with a partner at half speed. The next logical progression is to perform the engagement set at full speed on a pell with functional weapons (i.e., live steel). The goal is to provide the student with knowledge of how the weapon behaves during full-speed impact on a hard target. This is particularly important with the tomahawk because it is only under these circumstances that the need to retract the tomahawk on impact can be fully appreciated.

The training task conditions and standards for each of the aforementioned engagement sets are almost identical.

1. Perform the engagement set at slow speed, taking care to ensure that hands, arms, and legs are clear during each strike with the weapon.
2. Perform it at half speed focusing on smooth movement and transition.
3. Execute the set at full speed, focusing on accurate targeting with the weapons.

For brevity's sake, I did not include sequence drawings of the pell work. However, as an example, the next few pages demonstrate engagement set three being performed on the pell with the variation of a lowline attack.

**Action 1**

Face the pell within weapons range. Simulate the high parry while stepping across and delivering an angle 4 chop to the lower section of the pell.

**Action 2**

Swing the left leg around to the right
and deliver a highline slash to the pell.

4

**Action 3**

Retract the long knife and execute an around-the-head chop to the pell.

# ENGAGEMENT SET 4

**Task Title:** High block/parry, angle 7 chop, crossover, and horizontal slash

**Condition:** The tomahawk is held in the right hand in extended grip, long position with arm extended. The long knife is in the left hand in reverse grip.

**Execution:**

1. As a solo set
   a. Execute the high block/parry against an incoming angle 1 cut. Simultaneously swing the left leg backward, circling to the left out of the opponent's line of attack.
   b. Following the circular path begun with the block/parry, continue through into an angle 7 chop to the opponent's groin.
   c. Shift the hips across to the right and execute a horizontal slash to the opponent's throat.

2. With a training partner
   a. The opponent training partner should be equipped with a cuttoe trainer. Both partners should execute this drill at least 10 times before attempting it half speed.
   b. The set begins with the opponent delivering an angle 1 cut. You then execute a high block/parry while pulling the left leg around to his left side.
   c. Following the circular path of the block/parry, continue through with an angle 7 chop to the opponent's groin.
   d. Shift the hips to the right and deliver a horizontal slash.
   e. Standard: Repeat this sequence five times each training session.

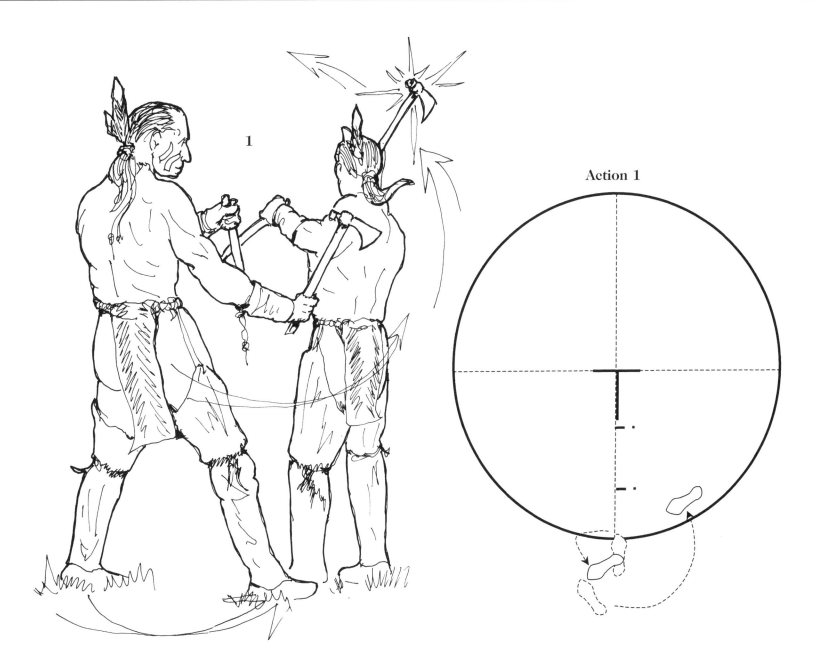

1

Action 1

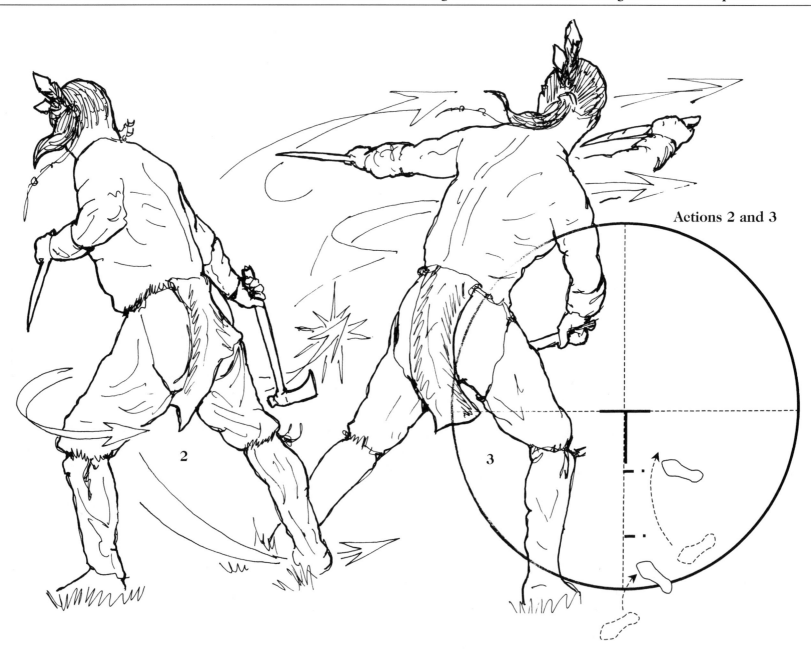

Actions 2 and 3

2

3

1

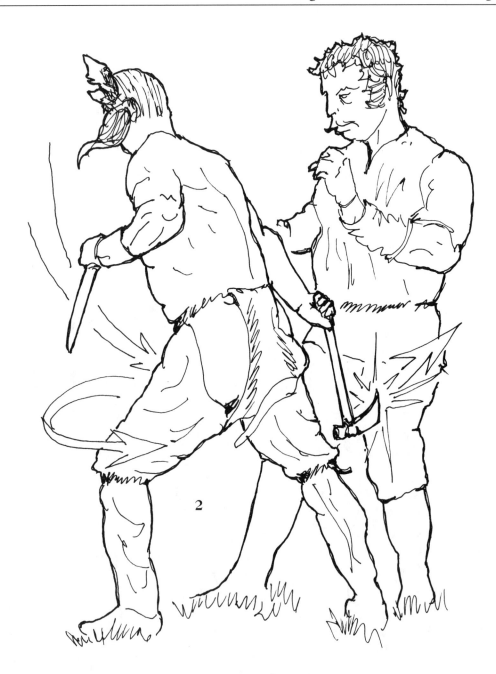

2

# ENGAGEMENT SET 5

**Task Title:** "Making the X"—side parry, angle 3 chop, angle 4 chop, and straight thrust.

**Condition:** Hold the tomahawk in the right hand, with an extended grip and the arm in a half-chamber. Hold the long knife in the left hand with a saber grip. The arm is slightly extended forward of the tomahawk.

**Execution:**
1. As a solo set
   a. Execute a side parry with the long knife and immediately deliver an angle 3 chop to the left.
   b. Follow immediately with an angle 4 chop to the right.
   c. Sidestep to the right and deliver an immediate straight thrust to the center.
   d. Note the footwork shifts on the following illustrations. Actions 1 through 3 are performed very rapidly, with the body shifting slightly off the opponent's centerline.

2. With a training partner
   a. The training partner should be equipped with a rapier or cut-and-thrust sword and dagger trainer. Care should be taken that both partners have adequate eye, throat, chest, and groin protection. Execute this set 10 times at slow speed before attempting at half speed.
   b. The set begins with the opponent delivering a straight thrust with the rapier. You then execute a high-side parry and shift to the left. Immediately execute an angle 3 chop to his right arm.
   c. Almost immediately the opponent executes a straight thrust with the dagger. You then retract the tomahawk from his right arm and execute an angle 4 chop to his dagger hand, turning his body to the right. Immediately follow by stepping out to the right and delivering a straight thrust with the long knife.
   d. Standard: Repeat this sequence five times each training session.

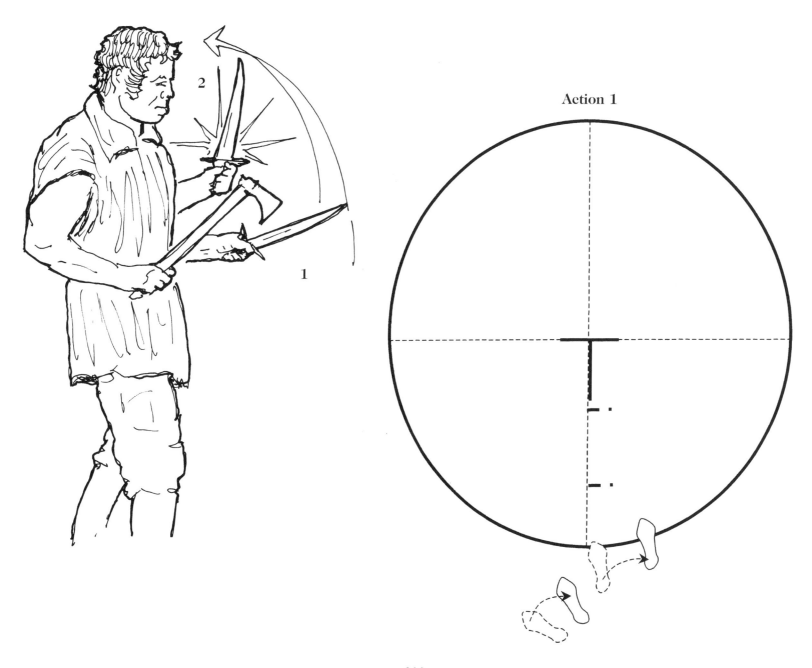

Action 1

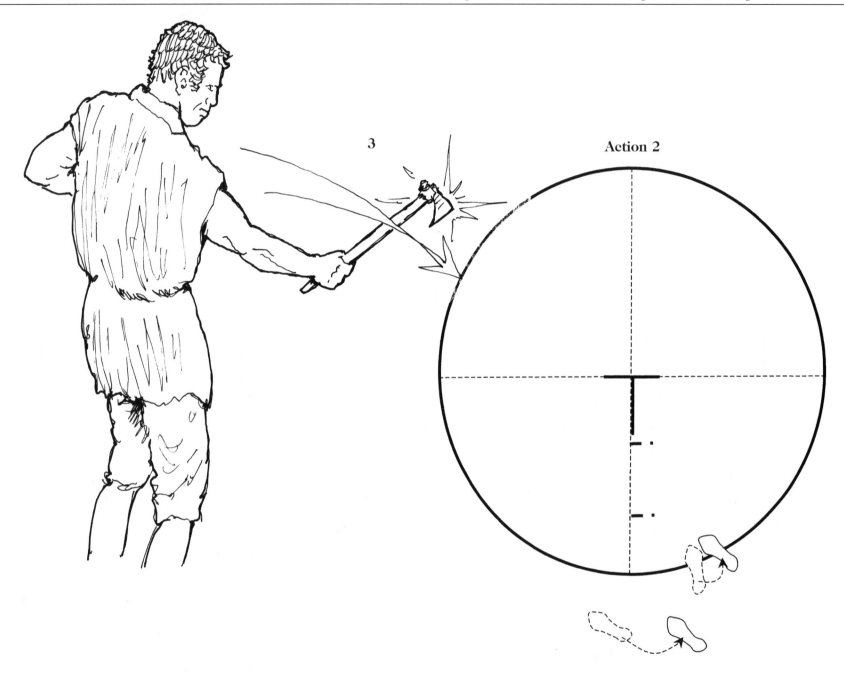

3

Action 2

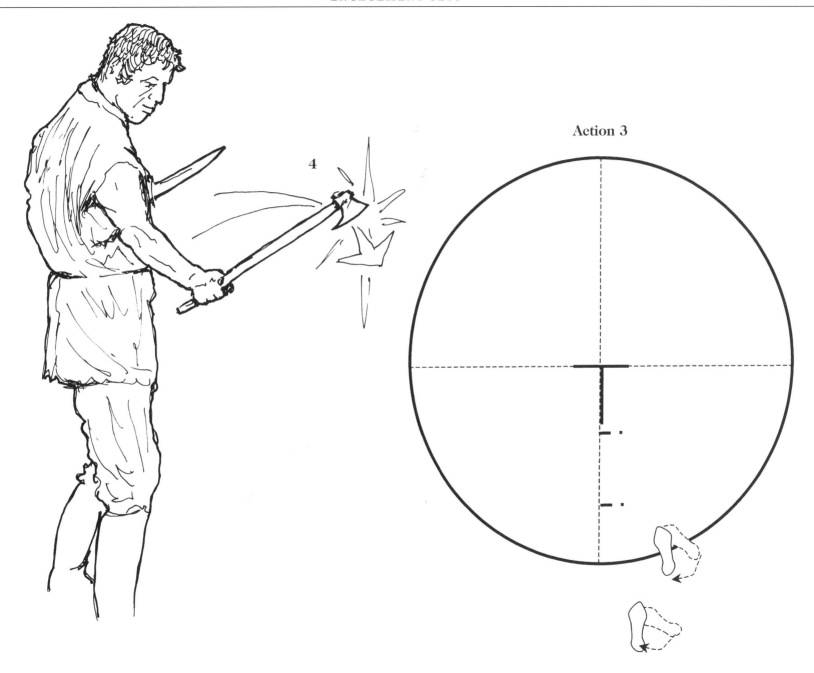

4

Action 3

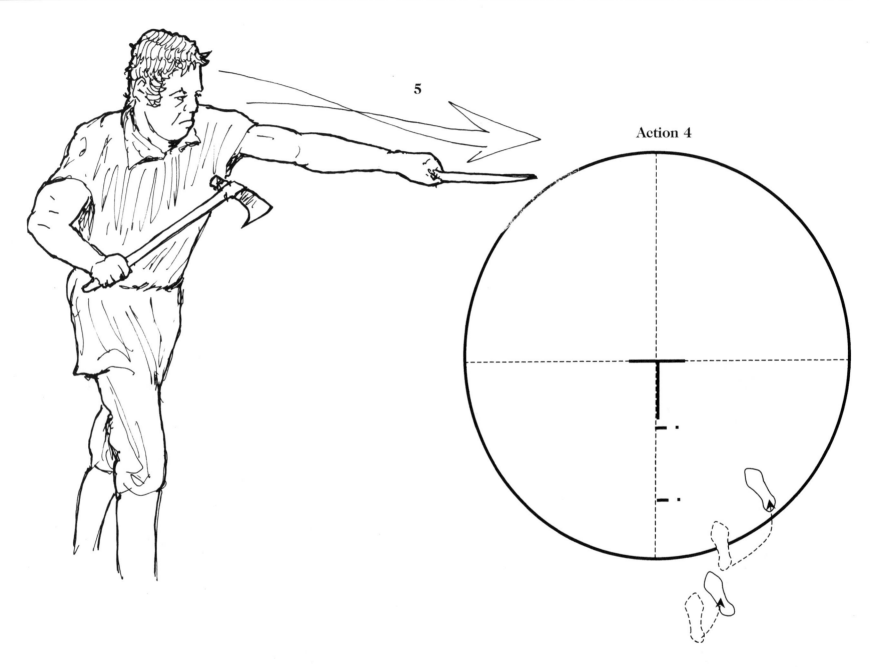

5

Action 4

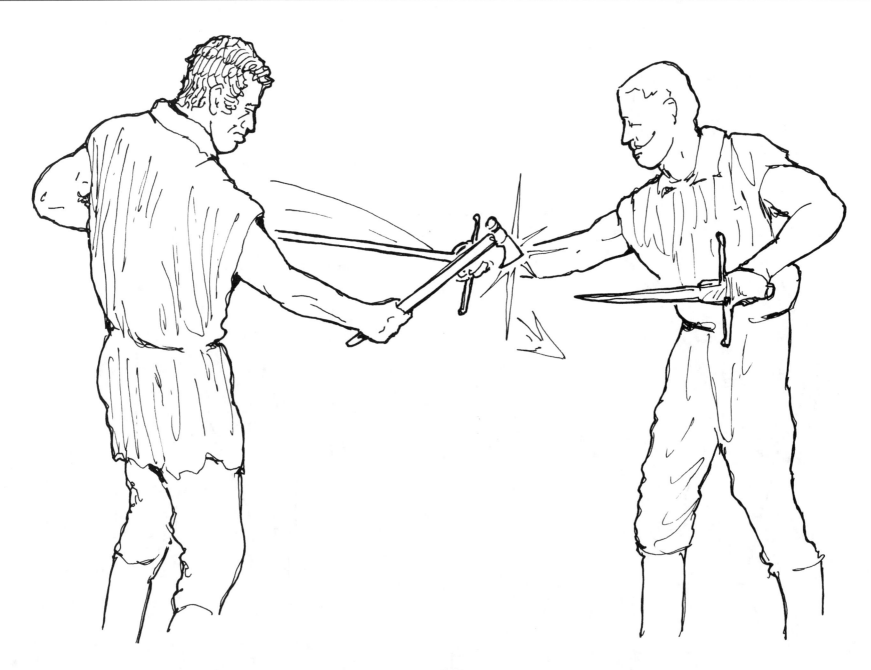

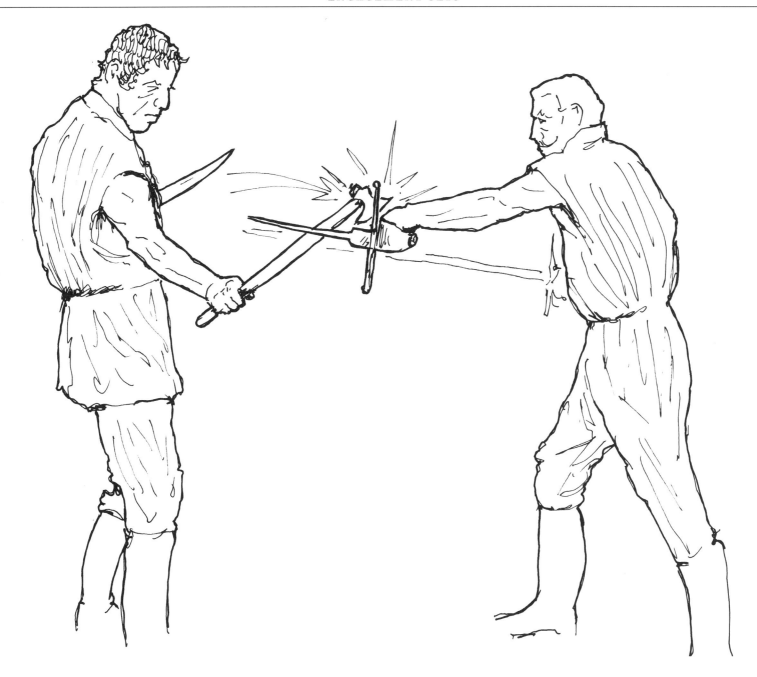

# ENGAGEMENT SET 6

**Task Title:** Two-handed block, left-hand grab, angle 8 chop, right pivot, and angle 7 chop

**Condition:** Hold the tomahawk with both hands in a mixed grip. Its head is to the left. Both arms are in a half-chamber.

**Execution:**

1. As a solo set
   a. Execute a two-handed horizontal block to the left.
   b. On completion of the block, reach under the tomahawk to grasp the opponent's weapon arm.
   c. Immediately deliver an angle 8 overhead chop.
   d. Pivot the left leg around to the right and slide to the opponent's side.
   e. Immediately deliver a reverse angle 7.
   f. Perform this set in a five-count movement, gradually increasing the speed of each technique until it flows smoothly.
2. With a training partner
   a. The training partner is equipped with a musket-bayonet trainer. Care should be taken that both partners have adequate eye, throat, chest, and groin protection. This set should be executed at least 10 times at slow speed before attempting it at half speed.
   b. The set begins with the opponent's delivering a long thrust. You then execute a two-handed horizontal block, pushing the firearm to his left.
   c. As soon as the opponent's gun clears, slide slightly forward, reach under his tomahawk, and execute a left-hand grab on his rifle hand, rifle, or arm.
   d. Immediately deliver an angle 8 overhead chop.
   e. On completion of the overhead chop, swing your left leg and body around to the right, sliding into the opponent's side or hip. Immediately deliver a reverse angle 7 chop to his groin or leg.
   f. Standard: Repeat these sets five times each training session.

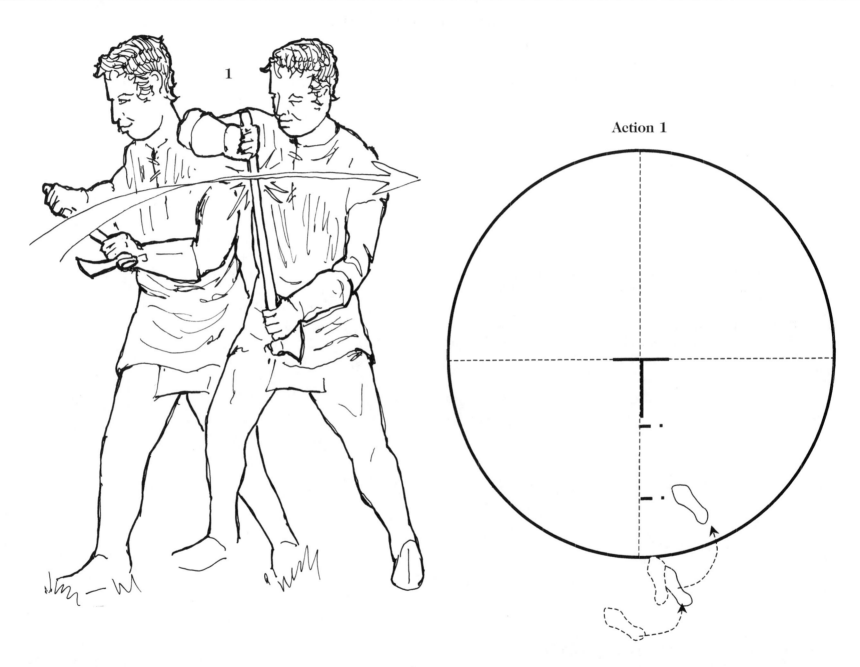

1

Action 1

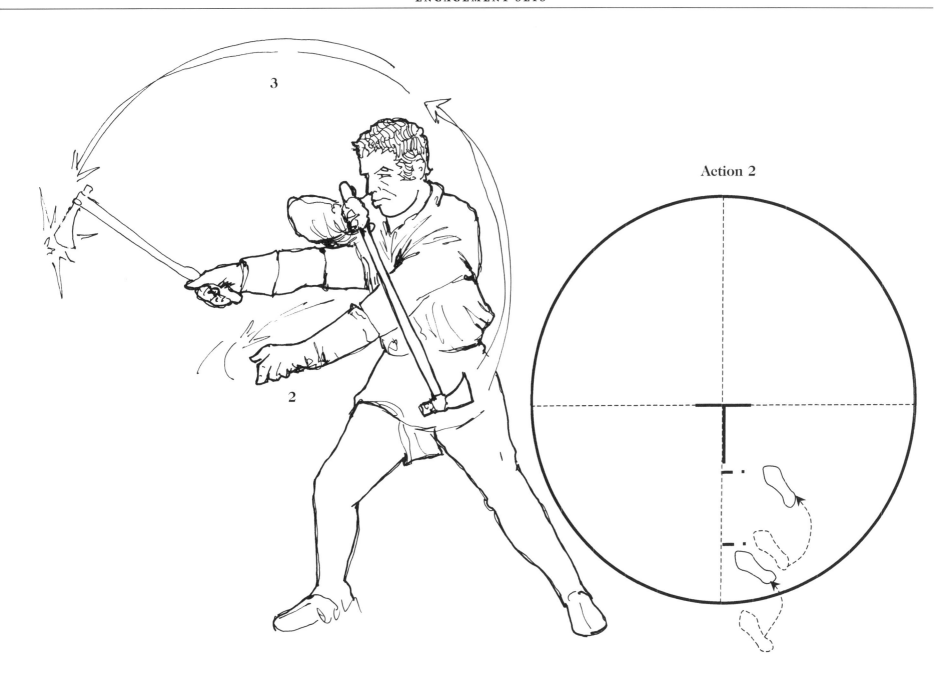

Action 2

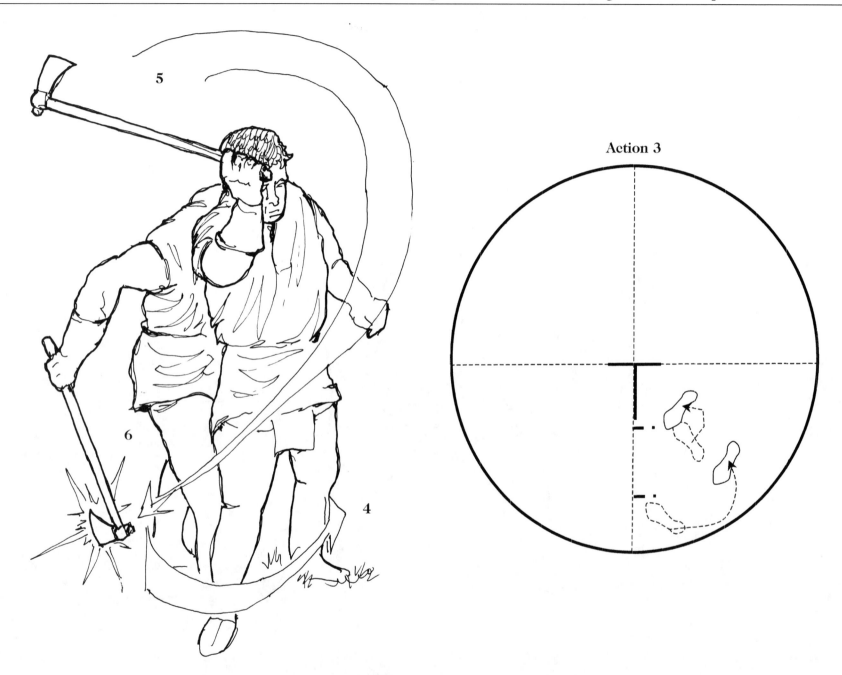

Action 3

# ENGAGEMENT SET 7

**Task Title:** Inside block, tomahawk catch and pull, straight thrust.

**Condition:** The tomahawk is held in the right hand; the long knife is held with a saber grip.

**Execution:**

1. As a solo set
   a. Execute an inside block with the long knife.
   b. Execute a hard pull-back with the tomahawk while delivering with a straight thrust or cut with the long knife.
2. With a training partner
   a. The opponent training partner is equipped with two long knives. Care should be taken that both partners have adequate eye, throat, chest, and groin protection. Execute this set at least 10 times at slow speed before attempting it at half speed.
   b. The set begins with the partner's delivering a straight thrust. You then shift to the left, away from the line of attack while simultaneously delivering an inside block.
   c. Once you have pushed his thrust off line, direct his tomahawk up and over his weapon arm (see enlargement) and execute a hard pull backward.
   d. Immediately follow the pull with a cut back to the left with the long knife.
   e. Standard: Repeat this set five times each training session.

1

2

3

Actions 1–3

# ENGAGEMENT SET 8

**Task Title:** Vertical rake, trap, and overhand stab

**Condition:** Hold the tomahawk in the right hand, the long knife in the left with a reverse grip. Carry both the tomahawk and long knife in a left-side position.

**Execution:**

1. As a solo set
   a. Execute a left-side draw with the tomahawk, slide forward, and continue to follow through to a vertical rake with a full choke.
   b. Immediately execute a downward rake and trap of the opponent's weapon arm.
   c. Bring the long knife upward from the left-side draw and execute an overhand stab.

2. With a training partner
   a. The training opponent is equipped with a war club. Care should be taken that both partners have adequate eye, throat, chest, and groin protection. Execute this set at least 10 times at slow speed before attempting it at half speed. Use a heavily padded tomahawk to prevent injury from the rake technique.
   b. The set begins with the opponent's charging forward, raising the war club to deliver an angle 8 strike.
   c. You execute a left-side draw to a vertical rake into the chin of the incoming opponent. Immediately pull the tomahawk over to the left and rake down, trapping his weapon arm.
   d. As the opponent's arm is trapped, draw up the long knife and execute an overhand stab to his throat.
   e. Standard: Repeat this set five times each training session.

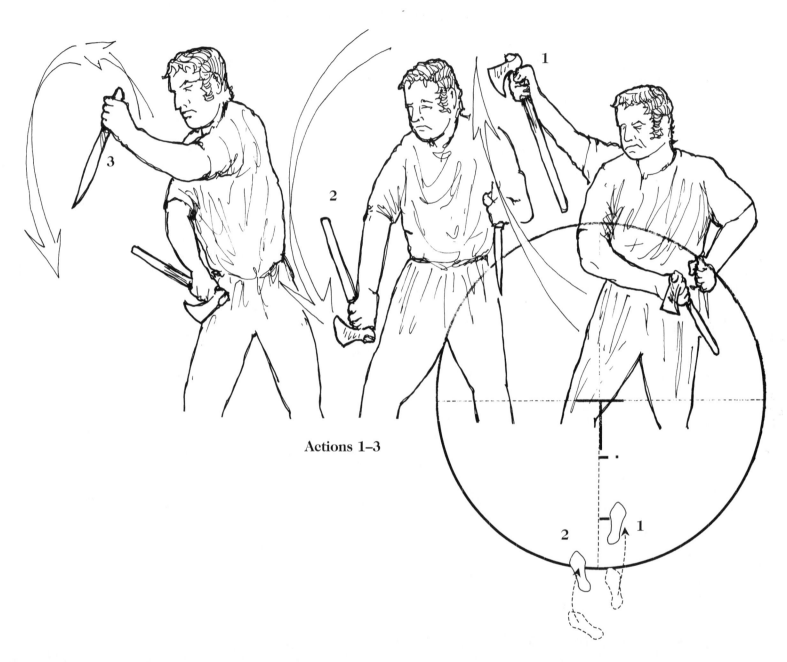

Actions 1–3

1

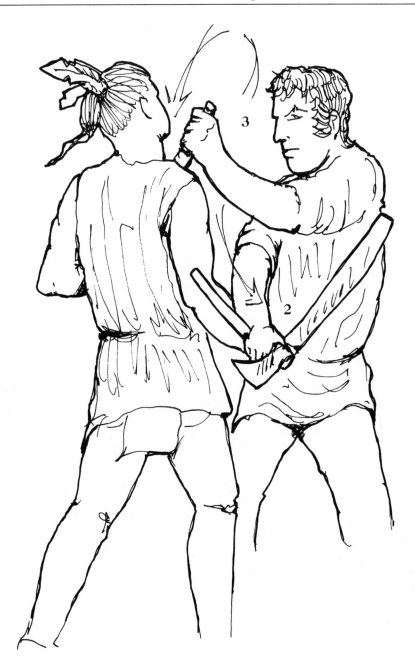

# ENGAGEMENT SET 9

**Task Title:** Vertical block, bridge, handle punch, and downward rake.

**Condition:** The tomahawk is held in the right hand and drawn from a right-side carry.

**Execution:**

1. As a solo set
   a. Step forward to the left and execute a right-side draw and deliver a vertical punch, blocking the incoming weapon with the tomahawk head.
   b. Immediately execute a bridge to the left and deliver a handle punch.
   c. Follow through into a downward rake while stepping back to the left.
2. With a training partner
   a. The training opponent is equipped with a war club. Care should be taken that both partners have adequate eye, throat, chest, and groin protection. Execute this set at least 10 times at slow speed before attempting it at half speed. Practice this set with a heavily padded tomahawk and war club.
   b. The set begins with the opponent's delivering an angle 8 strike with the war club. You then execute a right-side draw and with a full-choke grip deliver an immediate block of the war club with the tomahawk head.
   c. Execute a circular bridge to the left. As the handle clears the war club, use the handle to punch his face.
   d. Pulling the handle down, execute a downward rake along his body.
   e. Standard: Repeat this set five times each training session.

Actions 1–3

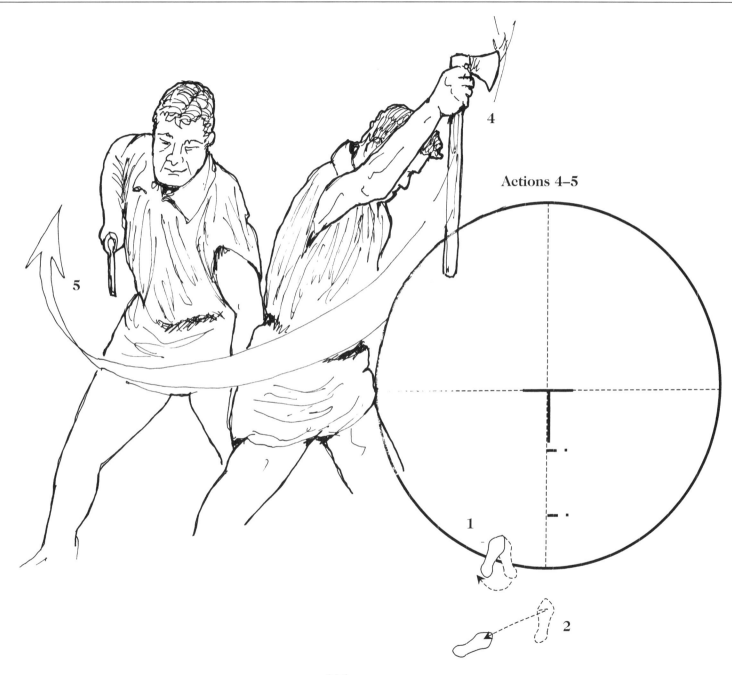

Actions 4–5

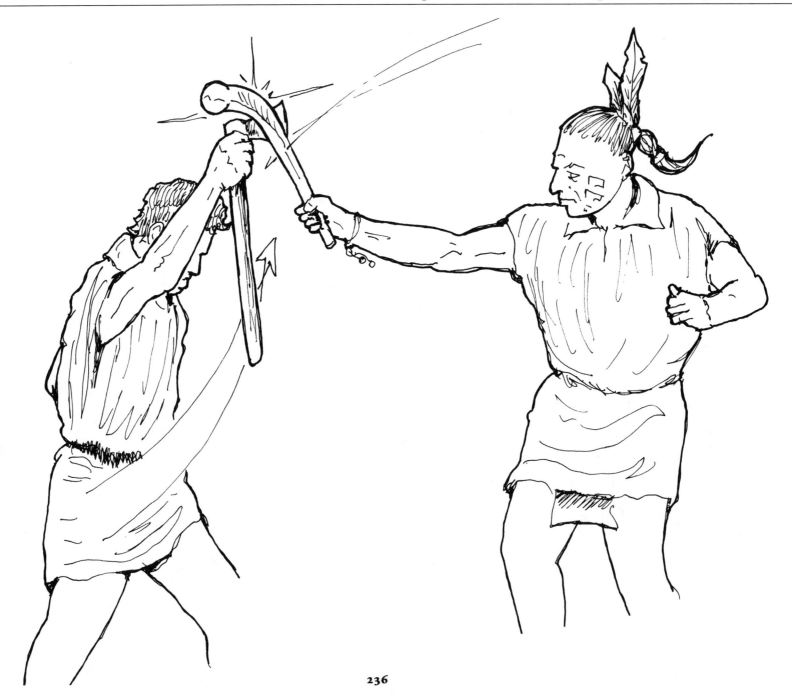

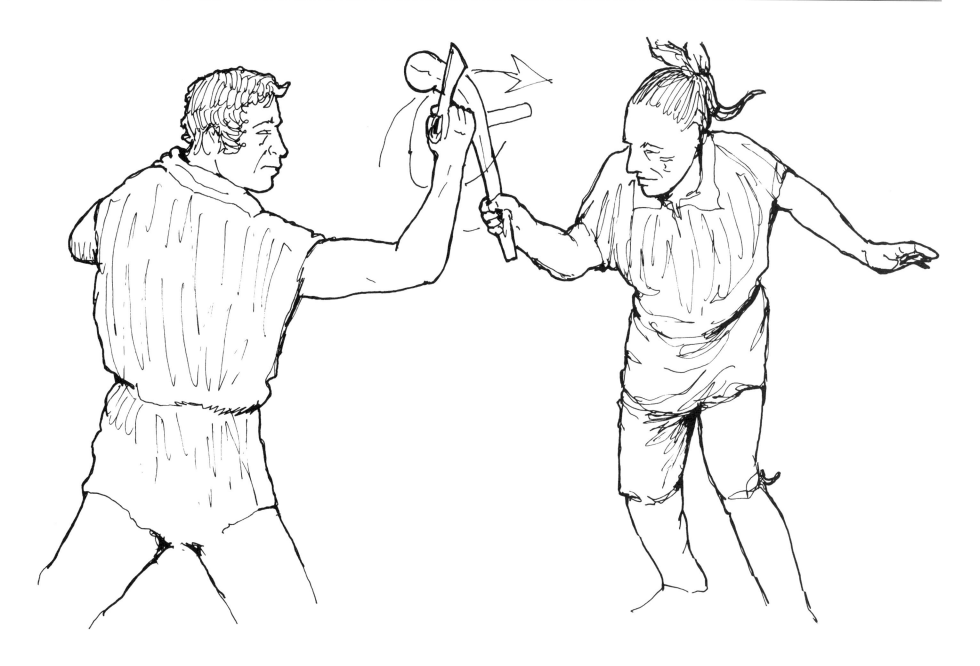

# Chapter 21

# Training Supplement 1– Solo Sets

The following pages contain four additional solo sets that can be practiced when a training partner is unavailable. The focus of these sets is to build aerobic endurance and timing. To build strength, you may wish to add 2- to 5-pound wrist weights when practicing these sets. As with the engagement sets, you should execute each set three times per training period: at slow speed, half speed, and full speed.

## SOLO SET 1

1. Execute a horizontal block to the left.
2. Follow immediately with an angle 3 chop.
3. Chamber the tomahawk back and execute a stab with the long knife.
4. Chamber the long knife back and execute a straight chop with the tomahawk.
5. Pull the tomahawk back, shift to the left, and execute a circular overhead chop.
6. Chamber the tomahawk back and execute a stab.

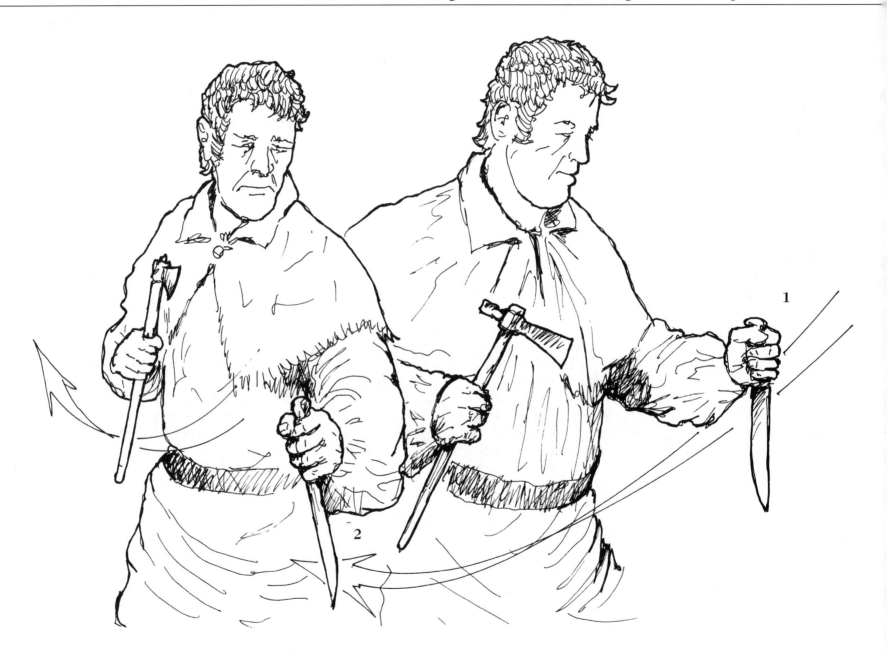

3

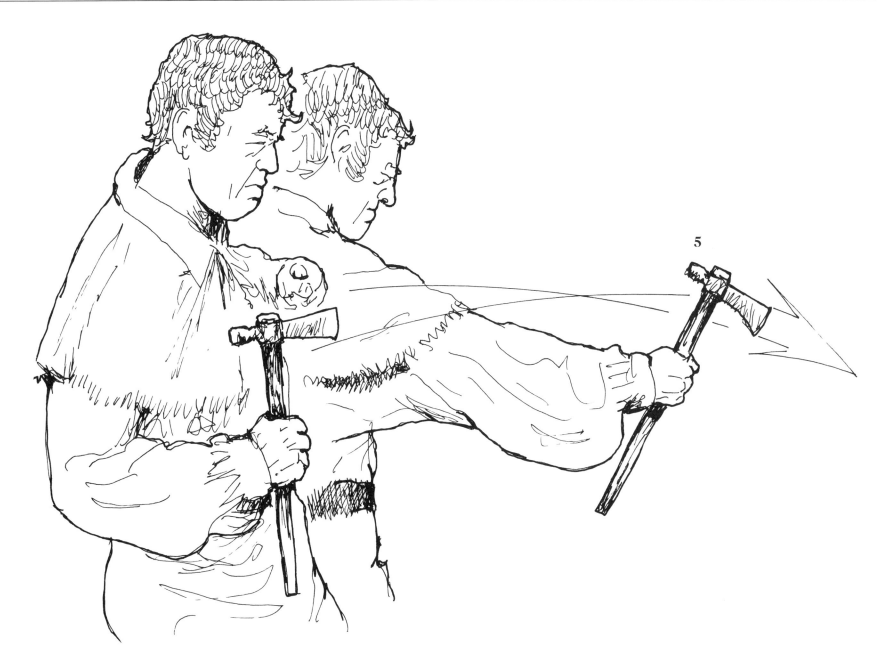

5

## SOLO SET 2

1. Execute a single-hand overhead block with the tomahawk.
2. Chamber the tomahawk and execute a straight thrust with the long knife.
3. Immediately execute an edge left with the tomahawk.
4. Shift to the right, pull away from the punch, and swing directly into a reverse angle 7 chop to the groin.

5

## SOLO SET 3

1.  Execute an angle 1 cut. Follow through to a stop and then execute an angle 7 upward chop.
2.  Pull the tomahawk back to a high guard and execute a lowline stab with the long knife.
3.  Pull the tomahawk back over the head and execute another angle 7 upward chop.
4.  Pull the tomahawk back down into a block-pull to the right, then up, and follow with a stab with the knife.

## SOLO SET 4

NOTE: For variety, I have included a tomahawk-and-saber combination in this set. Although there is no historical record that supports this combination of weapons, it does provide the opportunity to train with the tomahawk in a supporting role in the left hand.

1. Pull the saber up to a high guard and deliver a catch and pull with the tomahawk.
2. As the pull occurs, deliver a saber thrust high to the left.
3. Rotate the saber into a hanging guard to block the opponent's counter.
4. Execute an angle 3 (left hand) to the opponent's ribs. Immediately rotate the tomahawk to the left to deflect any incoming strikes.
5. Pull the tomahawk back to high chamber and execute a straight thrust.

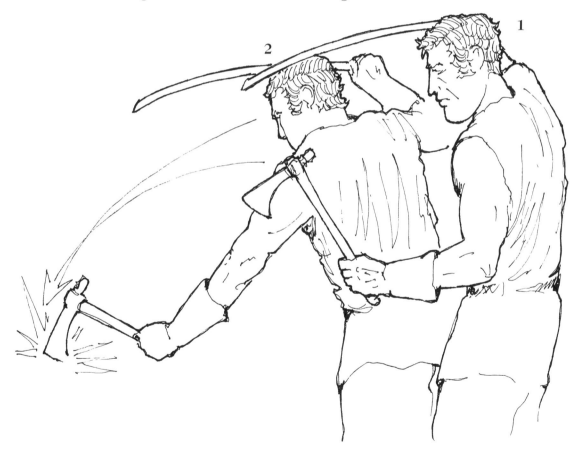

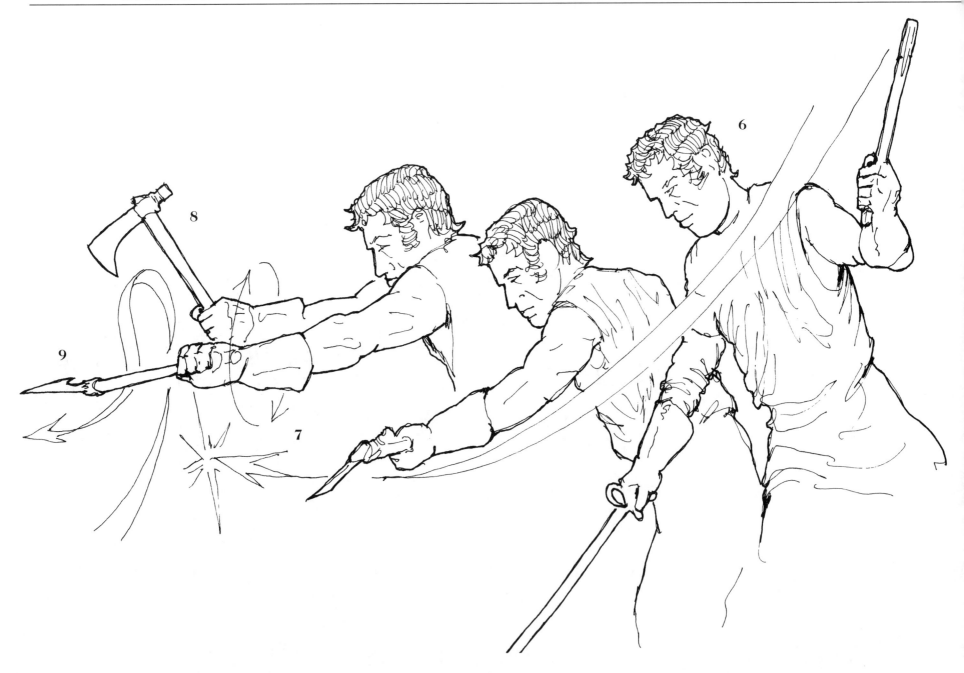

# Chapter 22

# TRAINING SUPPLEMENT 2– THROWING THE TOMAHAWK

No text on the tomahawk is complete without a section on its use as a projectile weapon. Unlike throwing the knife, which takes considerable training, throwing the tomahawk can be learned in a single session. In the space of a week, a person of average skill can become quite proficient.

Numerous first-person accounts from the 18th century document the throwing of the tomahawk by both the Indians and white men.

> *Morgan aimed a blow with his gun; but the Indian hurled a tomahawk at him, cutting the little finger.*
> —Alexander Withers, in a 1777 account

> *Moore had shot the chief, wounding him in the knee, but not so badly as to prevent him from standing. Moore advances toward him, and the Indian threw his tomahawk but missed him.*
> —Ramsey, in a 1776 account

> *[B]efore he could accomplish this, one of the savages approached and hurled a tomahawk at him. It merely grazed his head and then again took flight and seen got off.*
> —Alexander Withers, in a 1791 account

Along the early frontier of the 18th and 19th centuries, the art of tomahawk throwing was practiced regularly both for recreation and combat. This knowledge was passed down orally from generation to generation and was regular practice in some militia and military units.

Basically, there are two types of throwing: target and tactical.

## TARGET THROWING

Target throwing is done from a stationary position and aimed at a wooden target. The range is established, and all throwing is done from an upright position along a throwing line. Emphasis is placed on "sticking the tomahawk" into specific marks on the target, for which points are awarded. In many circles this is a very popular sport. Since this method is liberally addressed in numerous texts currently available, I won't dwell on it. Suffice to say that target throwing is the first place to start to learn proper throwing techniques, and you should spend considerable time throwing in this environment to achieve proficiency.

## TACTICAL THROWING

Tactical throwing requires training to throw in situations where you might be confronted by a foe. It involves the elements of drawing, evading, and throwing at a variety of ranges at wooden targets roughly the size of an actual opponent. It is this type of tomahawk throwing that I emphasize in this supplement.

### When to Throw the Tomahawk?

- Against multiple opponents moving toward you
- To disrupt or distract an opponent from attacking another person
- To gain time to employ another weapon or to take cover
- When you have more than one weapon—never throw a weapon if you don't have a backup!

### Which Is the Best Tomahawk for Throwing?

The correct answer is the tomahawk you use regularly. However, here are some specifics that constitute a good "thrower."

- Tomahawks with 3- to 4-inch edges make good throwers. Of course, this is a matter of personal preference, depending on how familiar you are with how a weapon performs.
- The handle of the tomahawk can be anywhere from 14 to 21 inches. Again, while this is a matter of personal preference, longer handles may require the use of both hands for a good throw. One absolute is that pipe tomahawks do not hold up well to repeated throwing because the hollow handle and pipe bowl are prone to fracturing.

### To Stick or Not to Stick?

It is very impressive to see someone throw a tomahawk and make it stick. It is certainly a valid goal for any tomahawk training, but in tactical throwing the focus is on hitting the target and basically knocking the hell out of the opponent. The ability to hit a target repeatedly at a variety of ranges is the first skill to be acquired before moving on to repeated sticking.

### Throwing Grip

Earlier in this book I addressed the use of the long extended grip, which is the ideal grip for throwing the tomahawk at most target ranges. The half-choke grip is also effective at ranges of less than 10 feet.

### Throwing Ranges

Most target throwing is accomplished at approximately 12 feet. That is a good distance to work with until you can consistently hit what you are aiming at. The next standard training range is 15 feet; then as proficiency increases, you move back to 20 feet. The ultimate goal for realistic engagements is between 30 and 50 feet.

### Methodology

There is no absolute method to describe the tomahawk throw. Most experts who throw at targets agree that the key to success is practice. All have their own methodologies to describe how they do it. What this really amounts to is getting the feel of the throw that works best for you. It appears to be a matter of instinctively estimating the range and then applying the correct force, trajectory, and release angle to hit the target. The height of the thrower and good hand-eye coordination are also key factors that

*enabled the boy to measure the distance with his eye, when walking though the woods, and strike a tree with his tomahawk in any way he chose.*
—Doddridge, in a 1768 account

### ELEMENTS OF A TOMAHAWK THROW

The drawing on page 265 depicts the tomahawk throw. Basically, the throw consists of four elements: toss, snap, descent, and impact. The toss involves moving the arm to the throwing position and swinging it forcefully forward to the release point. The snap is rotation that the tomahawk makes when gravity and drag cause the heavier head to drop steeply, "snapping" the lighter handle around. As this action is completed, the tomahawk descends and then hits the target. Regardless of the trajectory created by the power behind the throw, these elements are characteristic of most throws.

The drawing on page 266 depicts the arm action for the mechanics of the tomahawk throw. Begin in a stance with the right leg forward. Execute either a left- or right-side draw, moving the weapon to an extended grip in a long position. Immediately move the arm up to a high-guard position. Keeping the wrist as straight as possible, swing the tomahawk down with a slight extension of the arm. As the arm swings down, slide the right lead foot forward in a short advancing step while the trailing leg follows with a short slide forward.

## ELEMENTS OF THE TOMAHAWK THROW

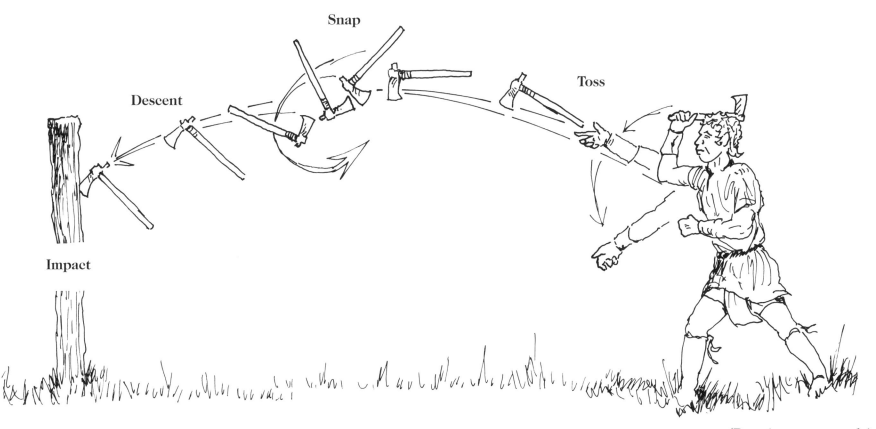

Snap

Descent

Toss

Impact

(Drawing not to scale)

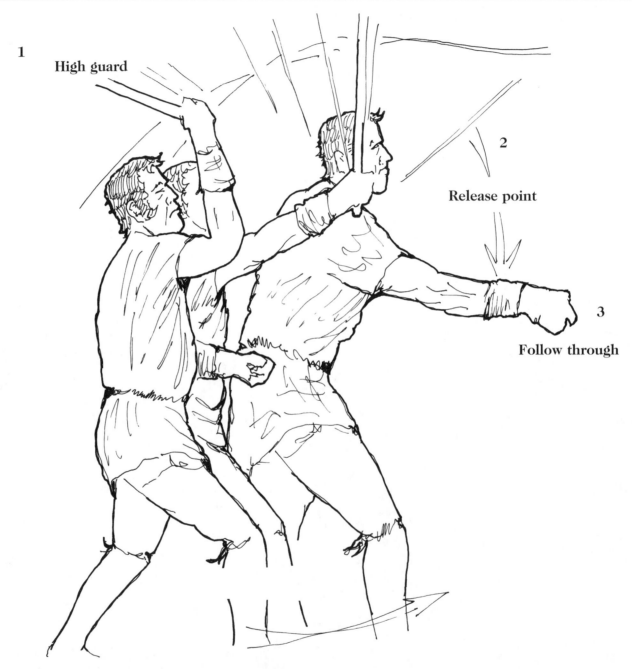

1

High guard

2

Release point

3

Follow through

This throw can also be executed from a position where you start with the left leg. Here the thrower steps forward past the left leg as the arm descends to the release point. The drawing below shows these foot-work options. During the course of any engagement, it may be necessary to move to avoid an opponent's throw or fire. This can be accomplished by sidestepping to the left or right before initiating the throw.

When confronted with a target or opponent, you must instantly estimate the range to the target and determine a release point for the trajectory of flight that the tomahawk will take into the target.

## TOMAHAWK FOOTWORK DURING A THROW

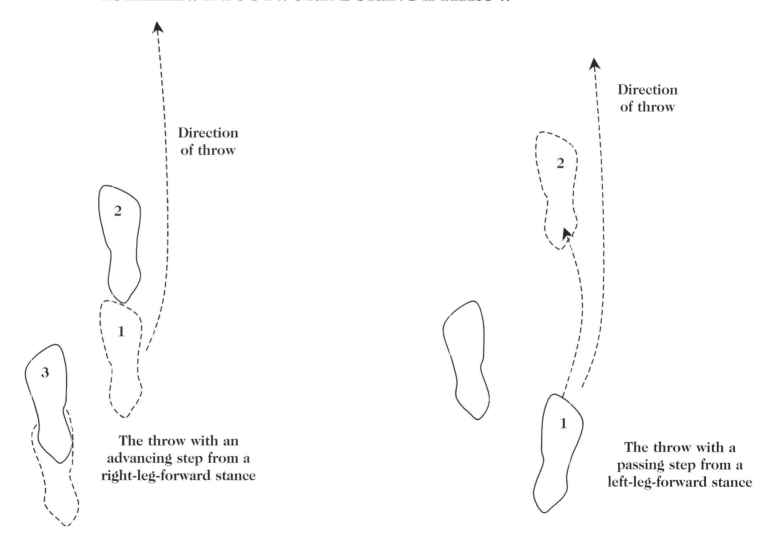

Direction of throw

Direction of throw

The throw with an advancing step from a right-leg-forward stance

The throw with a passing step from a left-leg-forward stance

# TOMAHAWK FOOTWORK DURING A THROW WITH LATERAL MOVEMENT OUT OF LINE OF FIRE

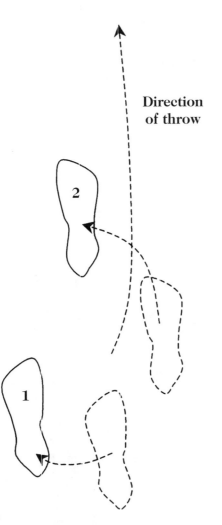

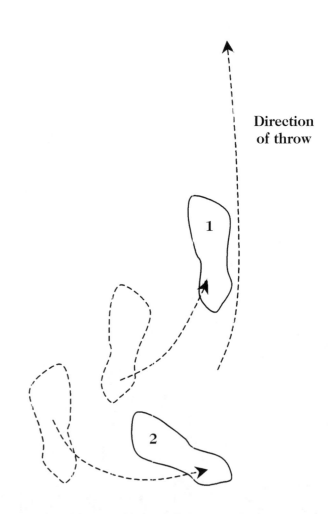

From a stance with the right leg forward, half-step to the left with the left foot and then immediately step forward with the right leg and throw.

From a stance with the right leg forward, half-step to the right with the right foot and then immediately swing the left leg around to the rear while executing the throw.

## VISUALIZING THE THROW

Lots of practice is required to throw a tomahawk accurately, especially at different ranges. To facilitate this, you should visualize a vertical line running from ground level to approximately 1 foot above the top of the target. During training you should study the general size of the target and release points on the vertical line for targets at 12, 15, and 20 feet. Again, it is the size that is the visual cue to determining the release point. The illustration below and the following training sequence expand on this concept.

## VISUALIZING RELEASE AND IMPACT POINTS

Release point

Impact point

Vertical line visualization

12 feet

15 feet

20 feet

## TRAINING SEQUENCE FOR THROWING THE TOMAHAWK

1. Look at the relative size of the target at 12 feet. Relate this to other natural objects in the surroundings. Trees or plants may serve as points of comparison in determining how large the target looks at this range. Visualize the line running vertically through the target and then focus on where the release point is on the line. Experiment with several test throws to verify the release point. Remember, the first task is just to repeatedly hit the target in the same general spot. Once this is mastered, then concentrate on "sticking" the head in the target. At 12 feet the release point should be around the middle or top of the head on the target. The impact area for this release should be either the neck or chest area. Note that at this close range, the trajectory of the tomahawk's flight will be rather flat with little arcing altitude. The snap will not be as evident as at extended ranges. Throws at this distance should be controlled, forceful, and fast. As proficiency increases, you will be able to target the head, neck, and abdomen rather easily. Practice this step three times a week with a minimum of 15 successful throws.

2. At a range of 15 feet from the target, repeat step 1. Note that throws at this distance require a release point slightly higher on the vertical line, usually about a foot above the head of the target. The arc of the trajectory and the snap are more pronounced as the tomahawk descends into the target area. At this range the throw does not require as much force as in step 1. It is best described as more of a tossing motion.

NOTE: In both steps 1 and 2, the tomahawk rotates only one turn before making the descent into the target. In the next step, the trajectory presents a greater arc and the tomahawk snap occurs twice.

3. Repeat the process in step 1 at a range of 20 feet. Throws at this distance require a release point along the vertical line approximately 18 inches above the head of the target. Remember that the tomahawk will snap (rotate) two times before descending into the target. An interesting tactical note is that in woods or heavy foliage, the airborne tomahawk tends to blend with the background, making it extremely difficult for the opponent to see it coming.

## OTHER CONSIDERATIONS FOR THROWING

### Targets Moving Straight Toward the Thrower

This situation requires you to estimate where the opponent will be after the moment of release. Here you are required to make the release point lower on the vertical line than if the target was stationary. The intent is to let the opponent's forward movement intercept with the trajectory—simply, he runs into the path of the tomahawk.

### Target Moving across the Thrower's Front

In these circumstances you are required to apply a lead to the moving target. Applying a lead involves using a release point slightly forward of the direction of movement. A general rule for targets at 20 to 30 feet is to apply a lead of about three fingers' width. For ranges of 20 to 15 feet, a lead of about two fingers' width is recommended.

## VISUALIZING RELEASE AND IMPACT POINTS FOR TARGET MOVING DIRECTLY AT THE THROWER

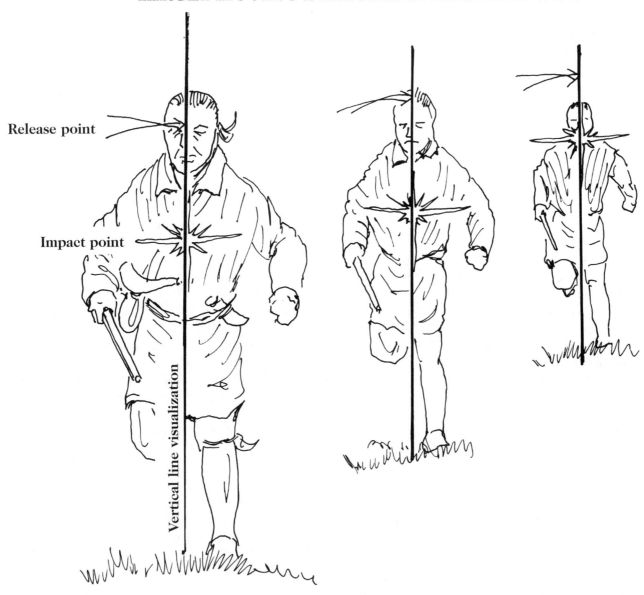

Release point

Impact point

Vertical line visualization

## VISUALIZING RELEASE AND IMPACT POINTS FOR TARGET
## MOVING ACROSS THE THROWER'S FRONT

20- to 30-foot lead

15- to 20-foot lead

# Chapter 23

# TRAINING SUPPLEMENT 3– SAMPLE TRAINING SCHEDULE

he following pages provide a sample 5-week training program for the tomahawk and the long knife. The schedule is based on the training tasks throughout this book, though not all of them are included. I included only the fundamental ones as a base for you to modify and develop your own plan. The tasks are arranged progressively in a weekly format so you can build on the skills learned during the previous weeks. Each task should be practiced in

sequence, as indicated on the schedule. In other words, the first week's tasks are added to the second week's tasks, and so on until you have completed the training plan.

Of course, this sample represents just one of the many combinations of tasks that can be developed into a personal training schedule. Remember that each training plan should end with mastery of one or more of the engagement sets in this book.

# TRAINING WEEK 1

### Goal: Develop proficiency in using the tomahawk in the right hand and the long knife in the left, delivering the cut, chop, and slash

**Task:**

- Execute eight-angle cut-and-chop flourishing drill using a wall chart or mirror. Repeat the drill five times each training session a minimum of 3 days a week.

  **SAFETY NOTE:** Before beginning the drill, make sure that the striking area is clear of personnel, furniture, and equipment. If training in an area with other partners, it is a good practice to announce "clear" before beginning the drill.

**Task:**

- Execute eight reverse-grip flourishing drills using a wall chart or a mirror. Repeat the drills five times each training session a minimum of 3 days a week

  **TRAINING NOTE:** For enhanced proficiency, switch hands and repeat the drill an additional five times. To increase speed and strength, use 2 1/2-pound wrist weights while performing tasks on alternate days. Concentrate on doing the drills slowly at first, gradually increasing to full speed. Use wooden or aluminum weapons at this early stage of training.

# TRAINING WEEK 2

**Goal: Develop proficiency in using the tomahawk in the right hand and the long knife in the left, delivering the cut, chop, and slash with live-steel weapons**

**Task:**
- Execute eight-angle cut-and-chop flourishing drill using a pell with an actual tomahawk. Repeat the drill five times each training session a minimum of 3 days a week.

**SAFETY NOTE:** Perform each angle of the drill very slowly at first, being certain not to move the edges too close to any of your body parts. Focus is on delivering technically correct and accurate cuts, chops, and stabs. Allow no personnel within 15 feet of the individual performing the drill.

**Task:**
- Execute eight reverse-grip flourishing drills using a wall chart or a mirror. Repeat the drill five times each training session a minimum of 3 days a week

**TRAINING NOTE:** Be sure to repeat the drills for week one as a warm-up before beginning this task. The last two drills should be practiced with live-steel weapons on the pell. When working on the pell, practice holding both weapons.

# TRAINING WEEK 3

## Goal: Develop proficiency in using the tomahawk and the long knife in delivering the rake, punch, and stab

**Task:**

- Execute four-angle rake drill using a wall chart or mirror. Repeat the drill five times each training session a minimum of 3 days a week.

- Execute a nine-angle punch sequence. Repeat the drill five times each training session a minimum of 3 days a week.

- Execute a tomahawk throw from a stationary position at a fixed target 12 feet away. Repeat the throw at least 15 times with focus on hitting specific points.

**Task:**

- Execute eight-angle stab sequence using a wall chart or mirror. Repeat the drill five times each training session a minimum of 3 days a week.

**TRAINING NOTE:** The four-angle rake drill should be executed with a draw from both left- and right-side carry positions, deploying both the tomahawk and long knife simultaneously.

**SAFETY NOTE:** Before beginning the drill, make sure that the striking area is clear of personnel, furniture, and equipment. If you are training in an area with other partners, it is a good practice to announce "clear" before beginning any drill.

# TRAINING WEEK 4

## Goal: Develop proficiency in using the tomahawk and the long knife in delivering base-deflection and edge-deflection techniques

**Task:**

- Execute a base- (then edge-) deflection sequence. Repeat the sequence five times each training session a minimum of 3 days a week. Perform the drill progressively at slow speed, half speed, and then full speed.

- Execute a base- (then edge-) deflection sequence against a training partner who is performing a six-angle attack with either a short sword, saber, or war club trainer. Perform the drill progressively at slow speed, half speed, and then full speed.

    **SAFETY NOTE:** Both partners should have complete head, eye, arm, groin, and leg protection.

**Task:**

- Execute blocks against eight-angle attacks using a wall chart or mirror. Repeat blocks five times each training session a minimum of 3 days a week.

- Execute blocks against a training partner delivering eight-angle attacks with short sword, saber, or war club trainer. Perform the drill progressively at slow speed, half speed, and then full speed.

    **SAFETY NOTE:** Both partners should have complete head, eye, arm, groin, and leg protection.

# TRAINING WEEK 5

## Goal: Develop proficiency in using the tomahawk and the long knife in combination with an engagement set scenario

Task:

- After performing the training tasks for weeks one through four, execute engagement set 1 (see pages 179–186) as both a solo set and with a training partner.

- After performing the training tasks for weeks one through four, execute engagement set 2 (see pages 187–192) as both a solo set and a set with a training partner.

# Chapter 24

# TRAINING SUPPLEMENT 4– APPLICATIONS FOR THE INDIAN WAR CLUB

**W**hen the word *tomahawk* is mentioned, often visions of Indians brandishing their weapons at full charge come to mind. As discussed earlier, the European traders were responsible for the introduction of the tomahawk, but it was the Indians' use of impact weapons that led to the widespread adoption of the metal hatchet, the tomahawk. Meanwhile, the Mississippian and Southeastern Woodland warrior societies continued to use the war club as their primary weapon. The war clubs were of four distinct types:

1. A 1- to 2-foot stick with a flint, bone, or animal tooth projection on the impact end
2. A ball-headed war club with 1- to 2-foot handle
3. The *atassa*, a 1- to 2-foot wooden sword shaped like the European falchion, the most prevalent design in the Southeast
4. A 3- to 6-foot spatulate, similar to Celtic leaf-bladed designs

Dr. Wayne W. Van Horne's thesis, "Warclubs and Falcon Warriors: Martial Arts, Status, and the Belief System in Southeastern Mississippian Chiefdoms," provides valuable insight into the use of various war clubs and Indian fighting techniques that were applied to the tomahawk. I can do no better than to quote from Dr. Van Horne's description:

*Further evidence of the importance of warclubs in Southeastern warfare is apparent in the analysis of skeletal fractures in burials at Mississippian sites 1 and 5. Evidence from these skeletal fractures shows that blows inflicted by warclubs to the head, clavicle, forearm bone (ulna), and ribs were a common form of trauma suffered by Mississippian warriors and were a frequent cause of death.*

From research such as this and accounts by European colonists and soldiers, we can assume that the Indian fighting techniques comprised combinations of angles 1 through 4 and angle 8 of the eight-angle attack sequence addressed earlier in this text. Dr. Van Horne's research also covers how descriptions of the warriors written more than a century apart show that there was a form of systematic training in the application of these attack angles:

*Garcilasco (of the De Soto expedition) describes the chief's demonstration in the following passage: "Rising to his feet [and] throwing aside his mantle of cat skin, which he wore as a cape, he grasped a broadsword (Atassa) . . . borne behind him by a servant as a sign of his rank, and leaping from one side to the other in the presence of the Cacique (chief) and the governor (De Soto), made many fine flourishes with a skill, gracefulness, and rhythm that greatly astonished our Spaniards. After sporting in this manner for some time, he paused with the sword still in hand, [and] approached the Curaca."*

Dr. Van Horne further comments on the 1701 account from English trader John Lawson, while Lawson was a guest of the Waxhaw tribe:

*Lawson describes warriors performing with Atassa warclubs, which he called "Falchions," at a feast given on the occasion of a visit by an ambassador from a neighboring tribe as follows: "Presently in came fine men dress'd up with feathers, their faces being covered with Vizards made of Gourds . . . in this dress they danced about an hour, shewing many strange gestures, and brandishing their wooden weapons, as if they were going to fight each other."*

Among all of the descriptions of the Southeastern warriors' use of warclubs in battle, these two demonstrations stand out for several reasons. For one thing, the two accounts are very similar, although they occurred a century and a half apart. This indicated a long tradition of warclub use in Southeastern societies. In both displays warriors performed prolonged and skillful ceremonial displays of warclub prowess in front of enemy delegations, indicative of a high level of training and social significance of warclub use. In both instances European observers expressed admiration of the level of skill of the warriors, and in both displays the atassa, or wooden sword warclub, was used.

# REFERENCES AND SOURCES

Addington, Luther. "Attack on the Evans Family—1779." *Historical Society of Southwest Virginia Publication* 3 (1967).

————. "Attack on the Ingles Family—1775." *Historical Society of Southwest Virginia Publication* 3 (1967).

————. "The Harmans' Battle—1772." *Historical Society of Southwest Virginia Publication* 3 (1967).

Bagwell, Bill. *Big Knives and the Best of Battle Blades*. Boulder, Colo.: Paladin Press, 2000.

Baker, Mark A. *Sons of the Trackless Forest*. Franklin, Tenn.: Bakers Trace Publishing, 1967.

Bricker, David. "George Foulkes—The Story of an Unsung Legend." www.earlyamerica.com (July 31, 2001).

Carroll, George. "Lewis Wetzel: Warfare Tactics on the Frontier. West Virginia." History Web site, vol. 50 (1991).

Conover, George S. (editor). *Journals of the Military Expedition of Major General John Sullivan Against the Six Nations of Indians*. Auburn: Knapp, Pect, and Thomson, 1887.

Digital History. "The Capture of Dieskau." www.digitalhistory.com (2002).

————. "The Battle of Bushy Run." www.digitalhistory.com (2002).

Durham, Keith. *The Border Reivers*. Oxford: Osprey Books, 1995.

Gorn, Elliot J. "'Gouge and Bite, Pull Hair, and Scratch': The Social Significance of Fighting in the Southern Backcountry." *Journal of Manly Arts*. April, 2001.

Gould, Kevin S. "Ambush at Oriskany." www.earlyamerican.com-31. July 2001.

Hassment, Corale (Web editor). "Doctor Thomas Walker's Journal (6 March 1749–13 July 1750): The Land of Our Ancestors." TNGen Web Project History Presentation. November 22, 2002.

Hudson, Charles. *Knights of Spain: Warriors of the Sun*. Athens, Ga.: University of Georgia Press, 1997.

La Crosse, Richard B., Jr. *The Frontier Rifleman*. Union City, Tenn.: Pioneer Press, 1989.

Laycock, George. *The Mountain Men*. Guilford, Conn.: The Lyons Press, 1996.

Louis, Ray. "Tools and Weaponry of the Frontiersman and Indian." www.pentimento.com. August 6, 2002.

Mather, Increase. *The History of King Philip's War*. Albany, N.Y.: J. Munsell, 1862.

Neuman, George C., and Frank J. Kravic. *Illustrated Encyclopedia of the American Revolution*. Texarkana, Tex.: Scurlock Publishing, 1997.

Peterson, Harold L. *Arms and Armor in Colonial America 1526–1783*. New York: Bramhall House, 1956.

Petter, Nicholas. *Worstel-Konst*. Amsterdam: Johannes Janssonius Van Waesberge, 1674.

*Santa Fe Republican*. "James Kirker—The Indian Fighter." *Santa Fe Republican*, November 20, 1847.

Thompson, Lynn C. *Fighting with a Tomahawk*. Coldsteel.com (December 6, 1999).

Van Horne, Wayne. "Warclubs and Falcon Warriors: Martial Arts Status and the Belief System in Southeastern Mississippian Chiefdom." Paper presented at Central State Anthropological Society, March 1993.

Wilbur, Keith C. *The Revolutionary War Soldier*. Guilford, Conn.: Globe Pequot Press, 1993.

Withers, Alexander, and Reuben Gold Thwaites. *Chronicles of Border Warfare*. (Originally published in 1831.) Reprint, Parsons, W.V.: McLain Printing Company, 1997.